Penelope Hobhouse
On Gardening

Penelope Hobhouse On Gardening

Photographs ANDREW LAWSON

Watercolours JEAN STURGIS

FRANCES LINCOLN

FRANCES LINCOLN LIMITED
4 Torriano Mews, Torriano Avenue
London NW5 2RZ

British Library Cataloguing-in-Publication Data
A catalogue record for this book is available from
the British Library

ISBN 0-7112-0816-6

Designed and typeset in Caslon 10 ½ on 13pt
by Studio Gossett

Printed and bound in Italy
by New Interlitho S.p.A.

First Frances Lincoln Edition October 1994

9 8 7 6 5 4 3 2 1

Half-title page: *Cotoneaster, euphorbias,
acanthus and annual honesty, clustered around
the old well-head in the Cedar Court.*

Frontispiece: *In the western summerhouse
border in the Pool Garden, yellow-flowered
Moroccan broom, asphodelines and Jerusalem
sage mingle with blue-flowered irises in spring.*

*In gratitude to the National Trust
for allowing me to live and learn at Tintinhull*

CONTENTS

MY SORT OF GARDENING

FORTUNATELY, GARDENING is a continuous learning process. Every day spent gardening, every visit to a garden, every book read, and every plant planted, for oneself or as part of a scheme for others, add to experience. These different bits of knowledge shape the way one plans, plants and dreams.

In making and looking after gardens – thinking out design schemes and using plants – there can never come a point when all the possibilities have been tried. Each site has its own individual advantages and problems, each plant will react a little differently depending on the conditions it is given and where it is put. Often features inherent in the site point in a firm direction. An open situation in a hot climate calls out for the welcoming shade given by old trees and by Italian-style pergola walks and arbours. Established trees and natural water demand gentle styling rather than a shift to formality; superb landscape surroundings need framing, not screening, while planting for privacy becomes more and more a priority not only in inner city gardens but also in much of the countryside. All planting success will depend on local and seasonal weather variations, the prevailing wind, frost pockets and rain shadows, all of which can play havoc with the best-laid plans.

Above all, gardens change as they develop. Plants grow and mature at different rates and their grouping and relationship to each other need constant revision. Plants grow out of their site or have a limited life span and need replacing. Even Capability Brown's groves of beech, shaped for appreciation two hundred years after his time, eventually reach a peak which is automatically followed by decline. Most of us plan for a few years ahead only, and few designers or amateur gardeners, except in the most formal of themes, can hope to

In the borders lining the cross path of the Kitchen Garden, Verbena bonariensis *flowers among roses and self-seeded* Malva moschata. *All the beds at Tintinhull are a mixture of shrubs, perennials, bulbs and annuals. This sort of planting was central to the garden philosophy of Phyllis Reiss, which I have inherited.*

allow for all eventualities. The more modest the scale the more frequently changes are made; in fact, a detailed planting plan is almost always altered by eye at planting time. A garden plan is not like an architectural blueprint, it can and must be revised as the garden is planted and begins literally to grow. It is not only the planning, planting and anticipation that make gardening enthralling, there is also the pleasure of changing and adjusting as the expected or unexpected happens. Watching a garden grow and having to adapt it each year makes gardening endlessly interesting. Next year can always be different and better.

Thomas Church, the great American designer who worked mainly in California, pointed out, in *Gardens are for People*, the difference between those basic principles of garden design which can be applied to any site, and the development of individual style, which remains a matter of taste. The former can be learned and put into practice. But the style which emerges, the combination of layout and planting detail, remains personal. Design ideas are quite different from principles, and it is the combination of the ideas with the principles that defines a style. The success of the style depends on its appropriateness to a site and on a fair degree of practical plant knowledge, both in choosing plants and in knowing how to grow them well. Each visit to a garden, great or small, adds to gardening maturity, and so does each gardening day or week.

More practically, Thomas Church defines the fundamental principles of design as unity – house and garden must flow together, linked by the repetition of hard or soft features; function – there should be a clear working relationship between house, garden and utility areas; simplicity – by which he basically means not having too many disparate ideas; scale – getting right the relationships between house and trees, hard surfaces and plants. This last is more difficult to define, but the best way to develop a feeling for satisfying proportions is by looking at good design wherever it is to be found, whether in houses and gardens or drawings and pictures.

To these prerequisites can be added the importance of attention to light and shade, closely related to scale and grouping: an open glade in a dark wood, a pool reflecting the sky above, light filtering through foliage and, as Sylvia Crowe says (in her *Garden Design*) 'the sudden blaze of sunlight appearing at the end of a chasm of evergreen' in an Italian garden. The colour and texture of plants act as further controls in garden design, influencing space and distance almost as much as perspective does. Flower colour is ephemeral, but the greens, greys, bronzes and purples of foliage add weight or lightness, close in a view or allow it to travel into the distance.

After many years of working as a gardener and designer I do now feel that I have developed a style which influences all my gardening efforts. It is tempting to call it the 'Tintinhull' style, because I learned it, in large part, from Tintinhull, the Somerset garden where I have lived and worked for the past fourteen years.

The garden at Tintinhull, which now belongs to the National Trust, was established, mostly during the 1930s and 1940s, by Phyllis Reiss, one of the great gardeners of the twentieth century. At Tintinhull I have been the decorator rather than the designer, using Mrs Reiss's inspired 'bones' – trees, walls and hedges and the framework of garden divisions – as the background to all planting.

Working in Phyllis Reiss's garden I have absorbed her sense of scale and structure and learned the importance of repetition in planting to prevent the restlessness produced by too much variety. I have had the chance to experiment further with her colour schemes and to develop some of my own idiosyncrasies in colour harmony. It has been at Tintinhull, above all, that I have really come to appreciate the idea of 'gardens within a garden'. For Tintinhull is a garden divided into a series of linked 'rooms', very much in the style of Hidcote and Sissinghurst, but on a more modest scale. The layout is essentially formal, constructed on a grid pattern, with lawns, paths and hedges all meeting at right angles. A main axis, a pathway of cut stone flags, runs from east to west along the south side of the garden. All the lateral compartments are hedged with English yew or surrounded by walls, while border areas are connected by a series of deep 'valves', pathways which lead through formal breaks in the flower beds. Borders and beds run parallel to the walls and hedges, which mark the boundaries and create the vertical barriers between the different sections and provide a backdrop for flowering plants. Tall trees – evergreen oaks, a cedar of Lebanon and a colonnade of old yews – balance with the mass of the house and provide pockets of alternating shade and sunlight. (Soon I shall be leaving Tintinhull, and perhaps my clearest memory, when I do not live there any more, will be of the outline of tree shapes against the sky.) As at Hidcote and Sissinghurst, the detailed planting inside this structure is informal, with coloured flowers and leaves weaving patterns for different schemes.

The combination of geometric 'bones', which give definition and structure to a garden, and free natural-style planting leads to a degree of informality. Sometimes the framework is so disguised by

Above: *The garden at Tintinhull is dominated by the old cedar of Lebanon. Here, its many trunks and tiered branches, distinctly outlined against the summer sky, are mirrored in the reflecting water of the pool.*

On pages 10–11: *The long view back towards the façade of Tintinhull House, through the symmetrically arranged foliage plants flanking the axis path that links the 'rooms' on the south side of the garden.*

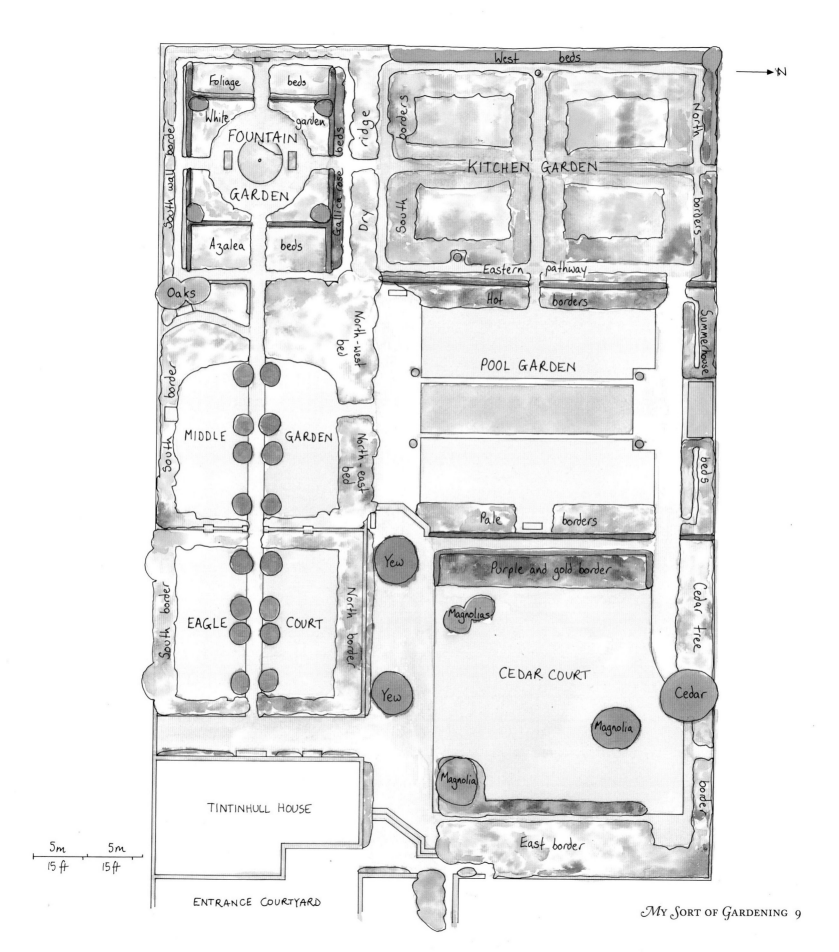

West beds

North borders

'N

Foliage beds

White garden

FOUNTAIN GARDEN

South wall border

ridge

borders

KITCHEN GARDEN

North beds

Gallica rose beds

Azalea beds

Dry

South

Oaks

South border

North-west bed

Eastern pathway

Hot borders

MIDDLE GARDEN

North-east bed

POOL GARDEN

Summerhouse

beds

EAGLE COURT

South border

North border

Pale borders

Yew

Purple and gold border

Cedar tree

Magnolias

Yew

CEDAR COURT

Magnolia

Cedar

Magnolia

border

TINTINHULL HOUSE

5m 5m
15ft 15ft

East border

ENTRANCE COURTYARD

the cottagey planting style that it is no longer immediately obvious. Some people think of Tintinhull as a formal garden because of the strict layout, others believe that it is informal because of the luxuriant, almost jungle-like, planting. Vita Sackville-West described Hidcote as a formal garden with a maximum of informality in the planting and Tintinhull is an offshoot of Hidcote. Mrs Reiss lived near there before coming to Tintinhull.

Since I have lived at Tintinhull and come to appreciate the strict geometry of each compartment and how each room is linked to the next to make the whole an integrated design, the 'gardens within a garden' theme underlies all my thinking, on whatever scale I work. This is true whether a design is formal or informal – the idea of separate garden compartments does not have to be implemented in geometric shapes. Although remaining a traditionalist at heart, I have found that, even in the most informal gardens, I can create rooms which reflect different moods, making use of the whole ambience of the site, which, in the end, is what matters.

I have taken Tintinhull as a role model for some other gardens. A garden I designed in Michigan is very much in the Tintinhull spirit, although none of the features actually copies any at Tintinhull: in the Michigan garden, planting is designed to keep the eye on the level of a colonnade of 'Bradford' pears and on the avenues of crab apples which frame the centre, rather than on the distractions of neighbouring houses. In a much smaller garden at the back of a house in Campden Hill Square in London we divided the typical city space, which sloped upwards, into three horizontal 'rooms' – a flat courtyard, a terrace and an open circular lawn – all with distinct yet linked planting schemes. In a herb garden I designed for the New York Botanical Garden a formal central knot pattern is surrounded by borders very much in the Tintinhull tradition of mixed planting, with symmetry and balance being as important as plant varieties. In my new garden at Bettiscombe in Dorset, the basic layout, which is not unlike that of Tintinhull in style, though much smaller, simpler and less labour-intensive, is now nearly complete. The elements that compose the framework are in place. It awaits further planting.

Gardening at Tintinhull, working inside a strong framework, is much easier than gardening in a wilder situation, in woodland, by streams or in a naturalistic cottage garden. Structure is just as important in the more natural garden but it must be subtler and less obtrusive, more like painting than architecture. In place of geometry the more impressionistic composition depends on free-growing plant groups to provide visual structure and give background, height and balance. On whatever scale, from trees and shrubs down to low-growing groundcover, the character of the plants becomes more important; it is their sculptural quality and how they relate and contrast with each other that provide the background to the garden and actually construct the design. Building up layers of planting to make a coherent picture requires both an artist's talents and an expert's knowledge of plants and their individual needs and habits. My greatest design challenge has been a garden in Fort Worth, Texas, where steep slopes and contoured lawns made geometry impossible and I had to achieve an organized natural look using many plants with which I was at first quite unfamiliar. In Fort Worth the soil is highly alkaline and in any twenty-four-hour period temperatures can swing rapidly between extremes of cold and heat, so plants have a tough time. Getting the right plants to withstand the stressful climate was of vital importance, and I needed a lot of local horticultural advice before I could begin to compose pictures, even in my mind's eye.

So, Tintinhull has been a great inspiration. I have also had the good fortune to see a lot of other gardens, in the British Isles, in Europe and in the United States. My most important formative period was probably the 1970s when, before moving to Tintinhull in 1979, I visited many of the great Italian Renaissance gardens. I believe every gardener should have this experience, or if this is impossible should determine to study pictures and read about the philosophy behind the gardens. It was in Italy that I began to understand the use of three-dimensional as well as two-dimensional space and how it was employed to relate and balance with the mass of the house. These old gardens are basically laid out in a series of separate but closely linked rooms, with the central pathways and features aligned on villa doorways and windows and other architectural elements. On hillsides, terraces adjust levels and provide views to the countryside. Massive trees – evergreen oaks, pines and cedars, many of them two or three hundred years old – guard and shelter the villas, shaping the skyline and providing areas of shade to alternate with bright sunlight. Cypresses grown as specimens or as hedges, with both vertical and horizontal lines, provide sharp contrast with more rounded tree shapes. You do not need to know any history to understand the simple beauty of these gardens. Their patterns have influenced all our gardening lives.

In America many of the most intriguing gardens have been made to set off or flow with new buildings. The best of these have a haunting beauty quite different from the traditional Renaissance symmetries. One garden, the Bagley Wright garden north of Seattle, which I saw a few years ago, is constantly in my mind. A low concrete-and-glass house, designed by Arthur Erikson, lies in a forest clearing with a dramatic western view over and above Puget Sound, set off by a geometric reflecting pool where water flows imperceptibly over the boundary edge as if into the chasm below. On the eastern side, a meadow, contoured by Cornelia Hahn Oberlander, stretches back like a vast lake of light behind the house, a total contrast to the dark forest beyond. White daisies grow in the grass.

It is interesting, however, that the most successful formal garden of the twentieth century is also to be found in the United States, at

Filoli in California. Filoli is another garden designed as a series of rooms, and it is a perfect example of symmetry and careful grooming. Planting as well as design is formal and repetitive. Like the classic Italian gardens to which its layout is related, it is a perfect place to train your perceptions. The principles on which these formal gardens are based can also be applied to more naturalistically styled gardens where there is no obvious geometry. Once your eye is attuned to balance you can dispense with rigid symmetry.

Of course, I have also been influenced by books. For me both Thomas Church's *Gardens are for People* (1955) and Russell Page's *The Education of a Gardener* (1962) are a constant source of inspiration. I remember always how Russell Page, in his first chapter, stresses the

This garden on the Isle of Oronsay was designed to fit into the local landscape and to offer protection against battering salt-laden winds. A grid of hedges and hurdles safeguards the plants.

importance of interpreting the landscape in which a garden is set before attempting any gardening detail. For example, in a cliffside garden I was asked to design in Maine, the formal themes I usually prefer would have been inappropriate, so all planning and planting was done to extend the natural feeling, with groups of hardy evergreen spruce providing shelter from salt winds as well as framing vistas to the ocean.

I also frequently re-read Sylvia Crowe's *Garden Design* (1958), in which she vividly describes Phyllis Reiss's layout and planting at Tintinhull, comparing the enclosed garden rooms to an Islamic garden, which represents, for the devout Muslim, a terrestrial paradise, a foretaste of heaven to come. In 1990 I made something very like an enclosed Islamic garden in Austin, Texas.

So, gradually over the years, I have come to feel more certain not only of my own style preferences but also of my attitudes and philosophies. I like enclosures, framed views not vast panoramas, trees which shape the visible skyline and balance with a house, horizontal lines – especially hedges, edges of lawns and pools and pathways – which meet at right angles and reflect a general symmetry. I love soft planting and plant shapes, billowing curves softening the hard lines of paths or hedges, but I do not like pointless meandering curves, often introduced in a rectangular city garden plot to disguise the straight boundary lines. In a natural landscape curves work in association with the lie of the land, and relate to overhead tree canopies or follow the natural direction of a stream. (And in Thomas Church's famous El Novillero garden at Sonoma, California, the abstract shape of the swimming pool reflects patterns in the valley landscape below.)

Sometimes my gardening philosophy clarifies what I do not like rather than what I do. Far more jarring, to me, than any garish colour combination is the sight of plants with entirely different cultural requirements growing alongside one another. Appropriate planting is vital to the success of a garden: it is essential to choose plants which will not only do well in any particular spot but will also associate happily with any indigenous neighbouring plants. As an extension of this, I prefer on the whole to grow species plants. I find that new plant hybrids or cultivars, especially when bred for longer and thicker flower spikes, for particular colour effects, shorter stems (no staking), or extended flowering periods, tend to lose some of their subtle qualities. The peculiar grace of a plant often comes from its own natural colour and from the proportions between flowers, leaves and stem. None the less, especially as I continue to design in different climatic regions, I appreciate the plants specially bred to cope with difficult conditions. And, of course, there are many old favourites among hybrids and cultivars which, as vast improvements on the original type plant, one uses all the time.

Beth Chatto's first Gold Medal winning garden at the 1977 Chelsea Flower Show was a lesson to all gardeners. Silver and grey plants of Mediterranean type grew together on a well-drained bank, while moisture-loving plants were gathered around the margin of a pool. Yet in spite of her example there are still gardens at shows where acid-loving plants are displayed next to those which tolerate only lime, sun-lovers next to the shade-tolerant, drought-tolerant next to bog plants, almost, it seems, deliberately to confuse the uninitiated, who may believe that gardening is like that.

Opposite: *In this modern garden in Michigan, vertical alleys of crab apples and lines of 'Bradford' pears create areas of light and shadow as well as dividing up the garden into 'rooms'. The horizontal lines of paths and pool edge meet at sharp right angles and handsome pots are symmetrically placed to flank the pool.*

Below: *Lady's mantle, creeping campanulas and a crimson Gallica rose soften the hard lines of the steps between the Pool Garden and the Kitchen area at Tintinhull.*

Each plant should be envisioned as an individual mature specimen but also needs to be perceived in its subordinate position as a contributor to the whole garden picture. I find it useful to keep lists of plants with special qualities to which I can refer when I want particular effects. Deciduous shrubs such as berberis, corylopsis, deutzias, dogwoods, hazels, philadelphus and viburnums work well in a mixed border, sheltering low-growing spring bulbs with their canopies and allowing space for good clumps of perennials for the summer garden, as well as giving attractive winter structure. Evergreens such as box, winter-flowering mahonias, choisya and osmanthus are the sort of shrubs which unite a border scheme throughout the year. In a natural landscape small trees or large shrubs such as magnolias, dogwoods and, if the soil is sufficiently acid, stewartia, styrax and tupelos (*Nyssa sylvatica*) provide a variation in strong shapes. Accents or focal points can be provided by dogwoods with tiers of tabulated branches (either *Cornus controversa* 'Variegata' or *C. alternifolia* 'Argentea') and viburnums such as *Viburnum plicatum* 'Mariesii', with a dense spreading habit. Perennials with sculptural leaves provide scale and definition at a lower level and are not wholly dependent on flowering for their appeal: crambes, euphorbias, thalictrums, macleayas, eryngiums, Japanese anemones and hostas are among the most common foliage plants which give borders a long season of interest. Others, in contrast, have more spiky effects: irises, phormiums, sisyrinchiums and yuccas which in their turn set off low-growing bergenias or mounds of silvery artemisias.

All the planting at Tintinhull is mixed: trees, shrubs, perennials, biennials, annuals and bulbs cover the earth in each section, and unity of design is achieved by distinct colour schemes and themes rather than by massed formal planting. These schemes are as suitable for a natural-style garden as for Tintinhull's right-angled beds and borders. Except for occasional 'framed' beds for seasonal bulbs and annuals (as in my Michigan garden), or in cutting gardens, I almost always mix woody and soft-stemmed plants. At Tintinhull, usually, colour groups are repeated in each line of vision; here this helps to introduce an air of formality, but I find this kind of linking equally useful in the more undulating beds and contoured shapes of a wild garden.

All the planting at Tintinhull is very close, with no bare earth to be seen; annuals and bulbs are fitted in between the more permanent plants. Any bare space is thickly mulched. Plants, usually in quite large groups (of at least five), cover the soil and weave together in as natural a way as I can control. Not only does the close planting look almost jungle-like, but, by preventing weed germination, it reduces maintenance. In a more naturalistic garden the planting style is only an extension of this: larger drifts spread in abstract patterns in less obviously structured surroundings. Even a 'wild' site needs a design frame, a series of balances and matching shapes.

After design and planting have been considered, there remains a third element essential to success: the general health of the garden. Maintaining soil and plants in good condition is an ongoing process, but the foundations for vitality are laid in the earliest stages. Planting in unprepared soil or soil with perennial weeds, for example, is wasteful and unproductive. In the worst situation it may be necessary to give two seasons to providing adequate drainage, then digging, cleaning and mulching to ensure the best start for plants. It is not always easy to persuade clients new to gardening that so much preparation is vital. I am personally applying this lesson to my own new garden at Bettiscombe, in which the basic soil is almost unworkable clay. Mistakes of planning can be corrected later, but if planting is done too soon it will be difficult subsequently to dig and incorporate compost and grit to lighten the soil, and it can be impossible to get rid of perennial weeds. Many old gardens have tired soil in which the plants cannot take up nutrients, as essential humus-making organic mulches have not been regularly added. When I came to Tintinhull, the soil, although workable, had for some years had only artificial fertilizers and routine digging in of well-rotted compost was needed to restore it to health. Fortunately, we were able to incorporate quantities of compost as we renewed the planting in each area.

After many years of designing and working in gardens, I now feel that I can walk into a garden and make a quick analysis of its successes and failures from a design point of view. More practically, I can usually judge the garden's state of health. Such appraisal becomes much easier as judgment matures, but it is always difficult to make an objective assessment of one's own garden. Even the greatest gardens have some features that work well and others that work less well; sometimes gardens become restless or overdesigned, with just too many different features. While a formal layout is always easily interpreted, occasionally a more natural garden has a true atmospheric grandeur and yet resists rigid design analysis, the garden concept seemingly having developed without being made to a rigid plan.

Whether the effect sought is formal or naturalistic, a garden is not meant to resemble nature; all gardening is artificial. Just as a painter or a sculptor arranges shapes and colours, so the gardener assembles plants. The art of gardening lies in creating a composition that is truly satisfying.

In all the beds at Tintinhull the planting is mixed, with a spring emphasis on bulbs which thrive between deciduous shrubs. Aconites, snowdrops, scillas and invasive bluebells, with a few groups of dark tulips, successively carpet the soil in the purple and gold border of the Cedar Court, providing interest from the New Year until taller plants, shrubs and flowering perennials start to perform in May.

A wisteria, trained carefully against the Ham stone wall of the old stable block at Tintinhull, in full flower in May. Occasionally the buds are damaged by late frost, but most years the wall is draped with long purple racemes that make a magnificent display in the austere setting of the Courtyard.

A restrained approach
Planting up pots
Ceanothus and a few favourite evergreen shrubs

THE COURTYARD

I FAVOUR THE IDEA that the approach to a garden should be relatively austere: architectural, not flowery, giving little or no hint of what is to come in the garden beyond. Gertrude Jekyll wrote about this, suggesting that, as well as being quiet in its planting, the approach to a garden should, ideally, be on the shady side of the house. The full glory of the main garden, on the sunny side, should first be seen from inside the house itself, so that a relationship is established between the building, its occupants and the garden. Suggestions of the excitement to come may be fleetingly conveyed in advance; at Tintinhull a wooden door in the courtyard wall, left open always except in severe storms, allows a welcoming, comforting glimpse of the Cedar Court to the north of the house as one turns into the yard. Even a closed door offers an invitation to further exploration.

An arrival area (and especially an arrival courtyard), presents a special opportunity for restraint in planting. The decoration should be minimal: trees and shrubs trained into architectural shapes, free-standing or as clipped buttresses against walls. If there are flowers there should be relatively few different sorts. A wisteria can make a purple curtain in spring (as at Tintinhull), Virginia creeper clinging by tendrils to walls might provide a lush green surface in summer, with a spectacular display of orange and red in autumn. If a wall is in shade a climbing hydrangea, *Hydrangea anomala* ssp. *petiolaris*, or the related *Schizophragma hydrangeoides*, both with attractive lacecap greenish flowers, can smother masonry with a pattern of twisted stems, green-leaved in summer. If space allows, topiary evergreens or annuals might be regimented in pots or arranged in a disciplined patterned parterre surrounded by low hedges of box.

Of course, these are just ideas and must be adapted for any particular site. If the arrival area is on the gardening side of a house, the thinking needs to be rather different. Helen Dillon's front garden in Dublin, for example – a magical place, hardly separated from a tree-lined street – is full of delightful planting.

However, as a principle, the muted approach is well worth considering. Many urban and suburban front gardens where unity and simplicity should be the norm have too many features in them: a pond, a rockery, a weeping specimen tree, mounds of earth which mimic the contours of a landscape garden in miniature, different plants which give a spotty effect. A well laid out parterre with box-edged beds, planted with tulips in spring followed by summer and winter annuals, with more permanent massed lavenders or cotton

lavenders if in sun, or sarcococca in shade, would be much less fussy. The geometry of the parterre might be in some way linked with the architecture of the house.

In most regions of the United States the planting of the front garden, visible to passers-by and to the owner, is solved quite differently. There, without boundary fences between neighbours, flowing lawns planted with specimen trees link adjacent properties to give coherence to a whole street or neighbourhood. The only individual planting in the front may be under the house walls, where evergreens anchor the building to the soil and often grow tall to create desired privacy, leaving the opportunity for personal gardening styles to develop in the fenced backyards hidden behind. I find this democratic attitude to sharing the front landscape very attractive.

At Tintinhull an almost square courtyard, originally a traditional stable yard, reached through gates on the roadside, is now used as the approach for all visitors. (During the previous centuries a door in the lane gave access to the Eagle Court garden and main entrance hall.) This courtyard, surrounded by walls, is paved with old stone blocks, each about the width of a narrow brick (8cm/3in) but longer (30cm/12in rather than 23cm/9in). They have probably been in position for more than a hundred years, and were originally planned for horses, not motor cars. Larger stone flags cover an area next to the seventeenth-century mullioned façade of the house and make for smoother walking.

For hard surfaces tarmac and cement and man-made paving slabs, although durable and requiring no weedkilling, are the least attractive of materials. Stone flags, slate or cobbles are all much more interesting and desirable, and they can sometimes be obtained from reclamation sites at quite reasonable prices.

For more simple effects, local gravel – a surface often found in traditional kitchen gardens – can be edged with boards. I have used gravel at Bettiscombe for the arrival court, my utility area and paths in the walled garden. The honey-coloured surface looks both

The view into the garden at Tintinhull from the Courtyard. This narrow glimpse, framed by spreading cotoneasters and the branches of the magnolia beyond, gives just a hint of the profusion of planting to be discovered. The pots inside the doorway are planted for spring with lily-flowered 'Burgundy' tulips.

The little blue Anemone blanda *has proliferated under the mahonia in the Courtyard. Small spring bulbs – snowdrops, muscari, scillas, chionodoxas and different anemones – have spread through all the flower beds at Tintinhull.*

attractive and workmanlike. If there is space for a lawn, line it with narrow boards, stone or brick: this will reduce the hours spent edging the grass.

At Tintinhull the south-facing wall of the house, on the lane, has a sun-loving winter-flowering clematis (*Clematis cirrhosa* var. *balearica*). With deeply cut delicate evergreen leaves and nodding bell-shaped creamy-green flowers for many months – especially in a mild winter – followed by silky seed tassels, it always earns its position. The variety *C.c.* 'Freckles' has more open flowers spotted with maroon. A yellow Banksian rose (*Rosa banksiae* 'Lutea') flowers in spring and has to be pruned immediately after flowering to allow new growth to form and ripen sufficiently for flowering the following season. An old native silver birch grows unusually tall to tower over the courtyard. A vast wisteria (*Wisteria sinensis*) is trained on the wall of the stables opposite the gates. Pruned lightly at midsummer and again, more severely, in winter, it flowers without leaves in early spring. Pots of tulips followed by summer-flowering annuals flank the front and kitchen doors. Ideally that should probably be all, but another bed next to the road and a trellis to hide the oil storage tank give extra plant interest. A tall aspen poplar, *Populus tremuloides*, hides an electricity transformer, with mahonias (the Oregon grape, *Mahonia aquifolium*) and Japanese anemones spreading through the bed beneath it. A thickly set *Phillyrea latifolia* and the rare similar but smaller-leaved *Maytenus boaria* from Chile, both evergreens, give definition in winter. The scented white multiflora rambling rose 'Bobbie James', its large individual flowers with overlapping petals held in clusters, flowers at midsummer to smother the trellis.

A narrow pathway that forms part of the entrance area of this garden in Michigan is edged with a harmonious assembly of golden plants – a yellow hollyhock, golden-foliaged hostas, Lilium auratum *and* Berberis thunbergii *'Aurea'.*

Planting up Pots

PLANTS GROWN in containers for decorating terraces, courtyards and porches give any garden a feeling of luxury and extend its season. Evergreens followed by bulbs, pansies or forget-me-nots last through winter and spring and in summer plants – of a single sort or a mixture – can be massed to resemble an indoor scheme of cut flowers.

Placed singly in key positions, the pots themselves, full or empty, provide focal points: a pair can frame a doorway; in formal rhythms they emphasize and enhance a design. I seldom use small containers, preferring large, elegant pots

even in a restricted space. A small enclosed garden will benefit from an out-of-scale ornament. The most beautiful containers, in wood, stone, lead or pretty handmade terracotta (preferably frostproof), are expensive, but I try to avoid the flat, textureless surface of plastic or fibreglass. In certain situations tin, painted or weathered silvery grey, is as satisfying as grander materials. Beside the kitchen door in the Courtyard at Tintinhull I have three upturned rhubarb forcers which I fill with tulips for spring, followed by summer-flowering annuals. The illustration (*above*) shows an arrangement of *Argyranthemum* 'Pink Australian', *Salvia buchananii*, osteospermum and *Helichrysum petiolare*.

Soil preparation is important. At Tintinhull we make our own compost, and we find that a good mixture for general use is one-third each by volume of plain garden soil, peat (or a peat alternative) and coarse sand. We add water-retentive granules and

a slow-release fertilizer. But of course it is easier to use a ready-made compost, which can be bought to suit the requirements of particular plants.

Planting is a simple matter, but it is essential to make sure the plants are adequately watered before being transferred to their permanent home. I generally fill a wheelbarrow with water and soak the plants in it until all air-bubbles disappear (*opposite, bottom left*). This summer I planted the big pots on either side of the stable doors with an arrangement of blue verbenas, dark pink pelargoniums, paler argyranthemums, dark-flowered osteospermums, *Cosmos bipinnatus*

'Sea Shells', helichrysums and the pink-flowered *Anisodontea scabrosa*, surrounding purple-leaved cordylines. With containers as large (and as stable) as this I sometimes economize by putting polystyrene in the bottom to fill up some of the space; then I add compost to within about 10cm/4in of the rim. When doing a mixed colour scheme, I put in any large plants, such as the cordylines, then position the smaller plants, still in their pots, around them (*opposite, bottom right*). Once I am satisfied with the arrangement I take them out of the pots (*left*) and plant them. I always plant very tightly, starting in the centre and working outwards, leaving as little bare soil as possible. To finish off I add extra compost, bringing the level up to 5cm/2in below the rim (*below left*), then spray the whole arrangement with water to clean off any soil remaining on the leaves (*below*). Don't forget your pots once you have planted them – regular feeding and watering is essential throughout the growing season. We give annuals and quick-growing perennials a balanced liquid feed every two weeks.

Ceanothus and a few Favourite Evergreen Shrubs

Ceanothus arboreus 'Trewithen Blue'

AT TINTINHULL evergreen ceanothus, growing as buttresses against brick or stone walls, are a mainstay not only for their brilliant blue flowers carried in sequence between spring and early autumn but also for their strong vertical and structural quality. When I started to garden seriously it was with a passion for evergreen shrubs, which provide such solace in winter when other shrubs – albeit many with beautiful bark or twigs – are bare. Although I have since been distracted, especially while at Tintinhull, by the delights of flowers and colour, I still study the habit and quality of evergreens and enjoy their infinite variation in leaf shades, texture and shape, as well as their contribution towards the essential 'bones' of a garden. Together with trees shaping the skyline and the horizontal and vertical lines of hedges and grass, these shrubs are the most important plant ingredients in any garden.

Walled gardens are particularly suitable for the Californian ceanothus and, of course, for many of the other exciting evergreens from California, as well as those from the Mediterranean and the southern hemisphere. Walls, especially brick, reflect heat and encourage wood to ripen and harden: this not only means that the plant is more resistant to cold weather, but also makes flowering the following season more likely.

My experience of ceanothus began with the spring-flowering *Ceanothus arboreus* 'Trewithen Blue', which I first saw at Trewithen garden in Cornwall, many years ago. Large soft rich green leaves clothe strong tree-like stems and the flower heads are a clear blue. It grows happily facing west on a wall of the Courtyard at Tintinhull.

Forms of *C. impressus*, with small hard leaves on densely branched stems which can be trained espalier-like on a wall, flower in late spring. 'Puget Blue' has magnificent dark blue flowers emerging from almost purple buds. Another spring flowerer is *C.* 'Cascade', taller with an almost pendulous habit, weeping forward when tied back against the wall. With narrow leaves it has clear blue flowers. It has inherited characteristics from the hardy *C. thyrsiflorus* with paler flowers, which performs a little later, in midsummer, and has some white-flowered forms, besides the prostrate *C.t.* var. *repens*, ideal for draping over a low wall or being encouraged to spread out over paving. *C.* 'Burkwoodii' flowers twice, in summer and again in autumn, while *C.* 'Autumnal Blue' carries pale blue flowers from late summer onwards.

I especially like evergreens with unshowy – but often fragrant – flowers, and leaves with subtle shapes and textures. There are various osmanthus, such as *Osmanthus heterophyllus* and its coloured-leaf forms, usually translucent in young growth, as well as the dense *O. armatus*, with jagged-toothed edges to the leaves and scented white flowers in autumn, and the larger dense olive-green *O. yunnanensis*, with tiny ivory-white scented flowers in late winter. *O. decorus* (*Phillyrea decora*) has a solid look; a handsome spreading dark green shrub, it is suitable for trimming into topiary domes and a splendid alternative to box. The Alexandrian laurel, *Danaë racemosa*, is another good edging plant; a small shrub that will endure deep shade, it was popular in the gardens of the Italian Renaissance. Its flowers are insignificant, but in autumn it carries bright red berries above its glossy, curiously flattened leaves.

The Mediterranean phillyreas are also among my favourites. *Phillyrea latifolia* is a small tree or large bush with glittering and fluttering green leaves, rather like a small evergreen oak in general appearance. Known as the farmyard tree, it is an ideal complement to stone or brick. A specimen can be allowed to make a dense bush or trained on a single trunk to make a broad-headed tree. The small narrow-leaved *P. angustifolia* is also desirable; its long thin leaves are almost glaucous when young. Much grown in the seventeenth century for topiary, it can be trimmed almost as tightly as the dwarf 'Suffruticosa' box (although it is not so hardy).

The invaluable evergreen viburnums are discussed on pages 120–21. The evergreen hollies also really deserve a chapter to themselves: in this confined space I can only mention a few of the most special. The hardy American inkberry, *Ilex glabra*, with small shining green leaves on a compact bush and small black berries, should be seen more often. Requiring an acid soil, it is resistant to salt winds and is an ideal shrub for seaside as well as for inland gardens. On quite a different scale, the Chinese *I. fargesii* and the Japanese *I. latifolia* are tree-like shrubs with the largest leaves of all hollies, those of *I. latifolia* having serrated edges.

I. pernyii is easily recognizable by its triangular spined leaves.

For a seaside garden or one in a mild climate, daisy-flowered olearias, mainly from New Zealand, are desirable evergreen shrubs. They remain much neglected because they are temperamental, disliking fierce sun – they die of sunstroke – but needing light. They have a superb range of leaf types, from the holly-like *Olearia* × *macrodonta* to soft grey-green *O. phlogopappa* varieties from Tasmania. If the climate is not on your side, try growing them in containers. *O. traversii* has rich grey-green leaves densely covered below in white felt. It is quick and vigorous and used as hedges in the Scilly Isles. One of the

Azara microphylla

Olearia phlogopappa

hardiest is *O.* 'Waikariensis'. Silver-leaved with showy white daisies, it has survived many years at Tintinhull.

Some of my favourite evergreens are definitely for warm areas. The true myrtles (*Myrtus communis*) from southern Europe, as well as those from the southern hemisphere (including *Lophomyrtus* and *Eugenia*), are among the best tender evergreens. *M. communis* hardly needs describing, but *M. luma* from Chile, with flaking cinnamon-coloured bark, is distinctive. All adapt well, at least for several years, to being grown in containers. The bay rum, *Umbellularia californica*, with a strong pyramidal habit and leaves that are intensely aromatic when crushed, is highly desirable for a sheltered spot. And no garden that has a suitable climate should be without the lacy-leaved *Azara microphylla* from Chile, with yellow vanilla-scented acacia-like flower puffs in early spring. Also from Chile, *Drimys winteri*, growing naturally into a pyramidal shape but happy to be trained back against a wall, has translucent leaves and creamy-white scented flowers in early summer.

The box domes at Tintinhull stretch as an avenue through the Eagle Court and the Middle Garden. Flanking the main pathway of diamond-shaped flagstones, and clipped annually to retain their shape, the domes link the garden compartments.

Formal symmetry in a walled garden
Structural planting
Flowers through the seasons
Box and yew topiary
A passion for hellebores
Euphorbias in the garden

THE EAGLE COURT

WITH ITS BOX topiary and mixed planting schemes, the Eagle Court is the most formal of the gardens at Tintinhull. Occupying the area below the main west-facing façade of the house, it has a symmetry that balances the architecture. The horizontal expanse of terrace, grass forecourt and perimeter borders almost matches the vertical house wall in extent. It is an outside room, a three-dimensional space. The effect is accentuated by the two yews beyond the north wall, matching a tall crab apple and flowering cherry in the south border. Curtaining climbers and wall shrubs decorate the walls and add to the atmosphere of green seclusion.

In this garden there is an almost exact correspondence between architectural features and plants used as the equivalent of architecture. The symmetry of the walls is reinforced by the eight topiary box bushes down the centre and the horizontal shapes made by the green panels of grass. Although the perimeter borders appear to be planted informally, in fact there is repetition of blocks of shapes and colours, very much in Phyllis Reiss's style and conveying a strong design message. This sort of planning sets a rhythm for all the beds in the garden, through which formality, cloaked and almost disappearing in free riots of colour, binds each scheme together. For me, in designing for others and now in creating beds of my own at Bettiscombe, repetition without exact symmetry seems to provide an essential key.

Although the Eagle Court is a self-contained area – as are all the Tintinhull compartments – an axial path of York stone slabs, flanked, here and in the Middle Garden, by the avenue of box domes, leads from the front door steps westward right to the end of the garden, terminating in the Fountain Garden's arbour of clipped bay. The pathway was laid down during the First World War, and the box domes (*Buxus sempervirens*) were added in the 1920s.

The west side of the house dates from about 1720. As a classical addition to the farmhouse built a hundred years earlier, it almost doubled its size, as well as enhancing its elegance. For two centuries the Eagle Court was used as an entrance from the main approach lane. Visitors reached the front door from a side gate in the south wall. All the brick walls which mark the boundaries of the courtyard were built during the eighteenth century and may be contemporary with the façade. Stone eagles set back on gate piers frame the narrow entrance to the Middle Garden. Although the south-facing wall would have been especially suitable for espalier fruits, it is probable that little gardening was done here until Mrs Reiss's day. After 1933 she turned it into a flower garden.

Mauve and lavender abutilons, blue ceanothus, euphorbias and early clematis dominate the Eagle Court in spring. In the foreground is Abutilon × suntense, *probably the most beautiful of the garden abutilons hardy in our part of England.*

Structural Planting

Mrs Reiss planted this tea crab, Malus hupehensis, *in the 1940s. Flowering gloriously in May, it also acts as a host to schisandra and clematis, while under its canopy flourish choisya,* Itea ilicifolia, *hellebores, perennial* Lunaria rediviva, Anemone *'Prinz Heinrich' and bergenias.*

ALTHOUGH SINCE coming to Tintinhull we have had to renew much of the detailed planting in this area, the main structural plants – including the topiary box, the crab apple, the cherry and a large mahonia (*Mahonia japonica*) that flowers in January – are Mrs Reiss's original plants. One of her most successful combinations has been the partnership between a pair of shrubs, Mexican orange (*Choisya ternata*) and *Corylopsis pauciflora*, planted in both the north-east and the south-east corners. Both shrubs are tolerant of sun or shade so the pairs developed at almost equal rates in different conditions. Recently we replaced those in full sun, which had grown ungainly in the last years. The partnership in the north-facing bed (in the comparatively shady south-east corner by the door into the lane) still survives, probably now at least forty years *in situ*. The choisya is trimmed annually after flowering, to prevent its branches encroaching over beds filled with hellebores.

The less hardy evergreen abutilons, ceanothus, shrubby euphorbias and lavenders in full sun in the south-facing border all have relatively short lives. Besides being susceptible to severe frosts they are always vulnerable to wind turbulence, an unwelcome characteristic caused by the wall and funnelling through the narrow west entry, the path of the prevailing wind. In a typical mild wet autumn these quick-growing evergreens put on a lot of new lax growth which can be cut back by succeeding winter frosts, weakening the plants at least for a season. Needing little feeding, they might do better if starved in a more Mediterranean-type soil than we give them. Mrs Reiss did not grow euphorbias in the garden; these are our additions. They play an important role in these sunny beds, with blue-green linear foliage in winter and acid-yellow flower spikes over months in early spring, ideal to complement the bright blue of flowering ceanothus. She certainly knew them, for Margery Fish, her neighbour at East Lambrook Manor, was a euphorbia enthusiast, stocking many different species and varieties in her nursery. Perhaps she worried about the poisonous properties of the milky juice found in the stalks. If the climate is suitable I always use shrubby euphorbias in spring schemes, and add other less woody ones where possible. I like to combine the lemon-yellow of their flowering bracts with mauve flowers such as ordinary honesty or Byzantine gladiolus or with the lavender flowers of glaucidiums.

A further contribution we have made to this part of the garden is the twisting *Stauntonia hexaphylla* on the wall. Reputedly tender, this evergreen climber from Asia, with deliciously fragrant flowers in spring, rarely shows signs of frost or wind-chill damage. I first saw it at East Lambrook, growing over the Old Malt House. Another elegant evergreen, the *Itea ilicifolia*, is about twenty years old. It was here when we came and may have been planted as a replacement for one planted by Mrs Reiss.

These evergreens are accompanied by perennials which also keep their winter foliage. Throughout the year there are the contrasting leaf textures and different greens provided by hellebores, hart's-tongue ferns and leathery-leaved bergenias in the shady beds, and, planted in blocks beneath the stone eagles, evergreen epimedium (*Epimedium pinnatum* ssp. *colchicum*) with delicate yellow flowers at the end of March. All demand frequent manicuring, especially in spring, when frosted shoots, dead leaves and flower heads need trimming. If it were my garden I would replace the labour-intensive bergenias with masses of suckering sarcococca (*Sarcococca humilis* and *S. confusa*), to provide scent in the New Year and glossy foliage throughout all the seasons.

In full sun clumps of sword-like iris and silvery artemisias lighten the more sombre darker shades throughout the summer months. For closer viewing there are Japanese anemones with maple-like leaves, glossy rosettes of late-flowering toad lilies (*Tricyrtis formosana*) that shine in the shade between clumps of hellebores and, on the sunny side, the fern-like foliage of Jacob's ladder, the ordinary *Polemonium caeruleum*. There are ferns (*Polystichum setiferum* and its form, *P.s.* Acutilobum Group), happily accommodated in cracks between stone, brick or paving, and two different corydalis, the weedy grey fluffy *Corydalis lutea* and the desirable *C. cheilanthifolia*, everywhere.

The character of the whole scheme in the Eagle Court is dependent on its most formal architectural features: the central domes of box, with leaf colours and patterns that continually change as young shoots emerge and fade between darker leaves, and the patterns made by the green panels of grass which, mown and edged next to lichen-textured stone, dignify the horizontal space. Phyllis Reiss's layout of paving, paths and grass, combined with the verticals of trees, topiary and walls, creates a completely satisfying whole. Sometimes it is possible to believe that the more flowery seasonal events are unnecessary.

By late summer the holly-leaved Asian Itea ilicifolia, *happy in the north-facing border with the wind-protection offered by the crab, is a fountain of yellow-green catkin-like racemes composed of tiny scented flower heads. Nearby, the oak-leaved hydrangea,* Hydrangea quercifolia, *which performs best if tied back against a wall, provides autumnal leaf tints, as well as trusses of white summer flower heads. The woodland aster,* Aster divaricatus, *has myriad white stars for a six-week period in late summer.*

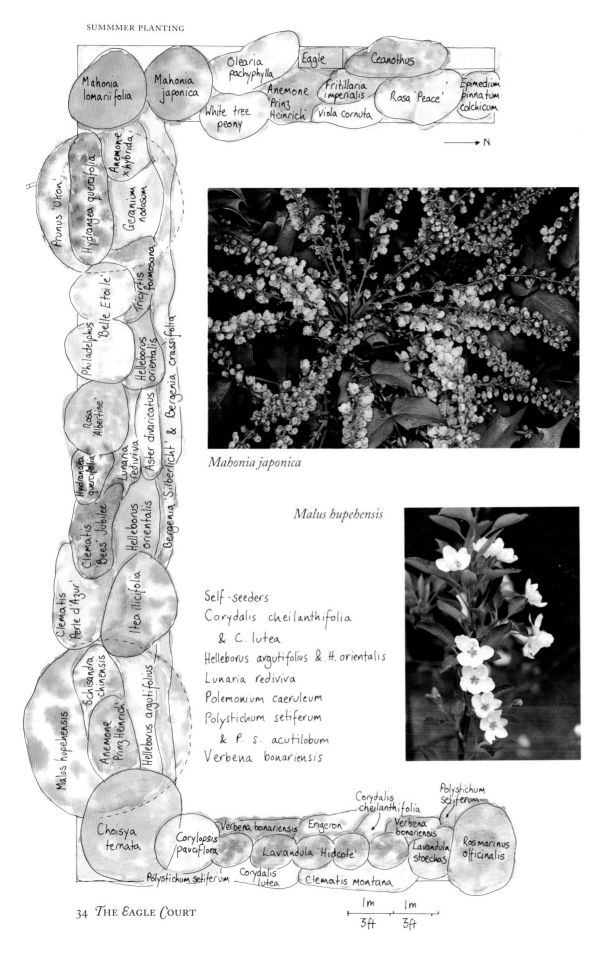

Mahonia lomariifolia

Mahonia japonica

Olearia pachyphylla

White tree peony

Anemone 'Prinz Heinrich'

Eagle

Fritillaria imperialis

Viola cornuta

Ceanothus

Rosa 'Peace'

Epimedium pinnatum colchicum

→ N

Prunus 'Ukon'

Hydrangea quercifolia

Anemone x hybrida

Geranium nodosum

Tricyrtis formosana

Philadelphus 'Belle Etoile'

Helleborus orientalis

Bergenia 'Silberlicht' & Bergenia crassifolia

Rosa 'Albertine'

Lunaria rediviva

Aster divaricatus

Hydrangea quercifolia

Clematis 'Bees' Jubilee'

Helleborus orientalis

Clematis 'Perle d'Azur'

Itea ilicifolia

Schisandra chinensis

Malus hupehensis

Anemone 'Prinz Heinrich'

Helleborus argutifolius

Choisya ternata

Corylopsis pauciflora

Polystichum setiferum

Corydalis lutea

Verbena bonariensis

Lavandula 'Hidcote'

Clematis montana

Erigeron

Corydalis cheilanthifolia

Verbena bonariensis

Lavandula stoechas

Polystichum setiferum

Rosmarinus officinalis

Self-seeders
Corydalis cheilanthifolia
  & C. lutea
Helleborus argutifolius & H. orientalis
Lunaria rediviva
Polemonium caeruleum
Polystichum setiferum
  & P. s. acutilobum
Verbena bonariensis

Mahonia japonica

Malus hupehensis

1m 1m
3ft 3ft

Rosa 'Peace'

Verbena bonariensis

Lavandula 'Hidcote'

Clematis 'Prince Charles'

Cestrum parqui

Ceanothus 'Puget Blue'

Polemonium caeruleum

Agapanthus africanus

Coronilla valentina ssp. *glauca*

Nicotiana glauca

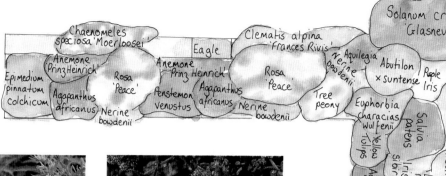

Solanum crispum 'Glasnevin'

Chaenomeles speciosa 'Moerloosei'

Eagle

Clematis alpina 'Frances Rivis'

Anemone 'Prinz Heinrich'

Rosa 'Peace'

Anemone 'Prinz Heinrich'

Rosa 'Peace'

Nerine bowdenii

Aquilegia

Abutilon × suntense

Purple Iris

Epimedium pinnatum colchicum

Agapanthus africanus

Penstemon venustus

Agapanthus africanus

Nerine bowdenii

Tree peony

Euphorbia characias Wulfenii

Staurtonia hexaphylla

Nerine bowdenii

Yellow Tulips

Salvia patens

Iris sibirica

Lilium regale

Abutilon × suntense

Agapanthus africanus

Yellow Iris

Salvia Sclarea turkestanica

Clematis montana

Salvia Cacaliifolia

Nicotiana langsdorfii

Iris sibirica

Agapanthus africanus

English lavender

Artemisia Powis Castle

Teucrium fruticans

Ceanothus 'Cascade'

Agapanthus africanus

Salvia Cacaliifolia

Nicotiana langsdorfii

Abutilon vitifolium

Euphorbia characias Wulfenii

Clematis 'Prince Charles'

Cestrum parqui

Lavandula angustifolia

Artemisia Powis Castle

Iris sibirica

Lilium regale

Polemonium Caeruleum

Yellow Iris

Abutilon × suntense

Salvia Sclarea turkestanica

Perovskia atriplicifolia

Clematis 'Bill Mackenzie'

Ceanothus 'Puget Blue'

Agapanthus africanus

Coreopsis Moonbeam

Yellow tulips

Nicotiana glauca

Coronilla glauca

Yellow hollyhocks

Rosa Helen Knight

Lilium regale

Clematis montana

Rosmarinus officinalis

Corydalis cheilanthifolia

Polystichum setiferum acutilobum

Lavandula 'Hidcote'

Verbena bonariensis

Corydalis lutea

Polystichum setiferum

Salvia patens

Ceratostigma plumbaginoides

Corylopsis pauciflora

Choisya ternata

Clematis montana

Clematis montana

FLOWERS THROUGH THE SEASONS

Groups of biennial Salvia sclarea *var.* turkestanica *in the Eagle Court have their stems tied together for support. This unconventional method of staking also works for tall crambes and verbascums.*

IN THE NORTH-FACING shady bed next to the lane, spring flowering opens with the cream or dusky purple flowers of massed Lenten hellebores (*Helleborus orientalis* of gardens) and the creamish-green flower cups and toothed leaves of the Corsican hellebore (*H. argutifolius*), below the still leafless crab apple and cherry. The hellebores start to flower early, the first blooms opening in bleak February periods, just as *Mahonia japonica* sheds its yellow racemes after weeks of scenting this part of the garden. They are at their most floriferous in mid-March.

By April the edging elephant's ears, *Bergenia* 'Silberlicht', produces almost white flowers. Overhead the best of all cherries, *Prunus* 'Ukon', with yellowish-green double flowers in April, is succeeded by the tea crab apple, *Malus hupehensis,* with scented white flowers opening from soft pink buds. Clematis (*Clematis* 'Bees' Jubilee' is an early flowerer, with *C.* 'Perle d'Azur' towards the end of summer) clamber through its canopy and twine in the

rambling June-flowering rose 'Albertine' and over the wall. There are many other possible flowering combinations between roses and clematis, and their habits and flowering periods make them especially suitable companions in gardens of any size. We added an unusual climber, *Schisandra chinensis*: it has pinkish-white flowers in early spring but, lacking a mate, does not produce fruit. All these scrambling plants perform much better and look tidier if helped by gentle teasing and tying-in. It is not enough to cut them back according to a rule book. Lower down, the perennial honesty, *Lunaria rediviva,* is one of the earliest perennials to flower, taking over from the Lenten and Corsican hellebores. It is a prolific seeder.

The larger wall shrubs are mostly spring-flowering. The white flowers of *Choisya ternata* appear in April, at around the same time as the flowers of *Clematis montana* and the primrose-yellow bells of *Corylopsis pauciflora.*

June-flowering *Philadelphus* 'Belle Etoile', with wide creamy flower petals, maroon-flushed at the base, is one of the best of the mock oranges. It grows happily in shade beside the oak-leaved *Hydrangea quercifolia*, the leaves of which colour sombrely in autumn. There is no space available in this bed for July flowers but by the end of August white-flowered starry wood asters (*Aster divaricatus*), with wiry black stems, flop over the edging of bergenias. We took this scheme straight from an illustration in one of Gertrude Jekyll's books (*Colour Schemes for the Flower Garden*).

In the south-facing border opposite, mauve-flowered *Abutilon* × *suntense* and *A. vitifolium* grow as pyramids between blue ceanothus (*Ceanothus* 'Puget Blue' and *C.* 'Cascade'), which are layered and tied back to give a flatter contrasting effect. When young these ceanothus are given winter protection with curtains of nylon net. They flower in spring, at the same time as the abutilons.

Beneath the shrubs, groups of yellow tulips – originally the scented 'Mrs Moon' but more recently, as these bulbs became

Species and cultivars of shrubby philadelphus scent the garden in midsummer. Philadelphus *'Belle Etoile', here in full blossom, grows in the half-shaded north-facing border above hellebores, perennial honesty and late-flowering asters.*

After flowering begins, the green twine is wrapped around the individual woody stems and zigzagged across to make an almost invisible cat's cradle.

difficult to obtain, the more vibrant-hued 'West Point' – are interplanted with clumps of June-flowering iris – an unidentified German type with lemon-coloured flowers – and hardy agapanthus, their blue flowers covering any possible August gap. Siberian iris with strong upright stems and leaves make architectural groups which when in flower extend the blue theme.

Although all this works quite well, the planting schemes in this border easily get out of hand and become a tangle of climbers and shrubs which spread out to weaken the growth and flowering performance of bulbs and low-growing perennials. The planting needs constant readjustment. Over the years, instead of tackling it as a whole, we have retained existing plants and added some for quick effects without allowing adequate space, bolstering up the scheme with late-flowering annuals in the prescribed blues and yellows. Probably the real problem lies in trying to imitate someone else's scheme without having exact plans or plant lists.

If it were my decision I would probably redesign the border adhering to the idea of blue and yellow but sharpening the colour effects with silvery leaves. I might well adjust the planting to include only shrubs and climbers for spring effects – ceanothus, abutilon, coronilla, corylopsis and choisya (for foliage as well as for its scented white flowers), with cream and yellow lilies and annuals, grown from seed and from cuttings from tender plants, contributing much of the summer colour. I would omit all perennials. This sounds labour-intensive, but it is the sort of gardening I enjoy and can do well. The blues and yellows would cover a broad spectrum from blueish-mauve to violet and from cream to purest primrose-yellow. Bulbs would allow me to bolster early-summer effects with masses of globular-headed mauve alliums to flower after the yellow tulips, followed in succession by blue brodiaeas, golden lilies (*Lilium* Golden Splendor) and regale lilies (both *L. regale* and *L.r.* Album Group), and separated by the strong clumps of existing agapanthus. The aspect

Biennial Salvia sclarea *var.* turkestanica *flourishes near* Lilium regale Album Group *in the south-facing border. Ideally this salvia, when it has finished flowering, could be replaced by pots of late-flowering bulbs – perhaps acidanthera (Gladiolus callianthus)* or *Galtonia candicans, the summer hyacinth.*

suits sun-loving blue-flowering salvias (*Salvia patens, S. cacaliifolia* and *S. guaranitica*), among the best and brightest summer blues. Annuals would include yellow and lime-green tobacco plants (*Nicotiana langsdorffii* and *N.* 'Lime Green'). To set all these off I would have the silvery *Artemisia arborescens* 'Faith Raven', its filigree leaf shapes shimmering near the back with *Senecio viravira*, and plant *Artemisia* 'Powis Castle' or *Lotus hirsutus* along the front.

For a border I designed near a swimming pool in the gardens at Royaumont in the Ile-de-France, I was asked to use mainly blue and grey plants. I included very little green foliage but concentrated on giving bulk and depth with grey-leaved shrubs. With more space at my disposal, I was also able to plant a background hedge of silvery sea buckthorn (*Hippophaë rhamnoides*).

To return to the Eagle Court at Tintinhull: in the corner between the north and west walls, the fast-growing *Solanum crispum* 'Glasnevin' is rampant and produces its blue flowers through most of the summer months. By mid-June the bush rose 'Peace', one of Mrs Reiss's favourites, is in bloom in the west border. It will flower again in September.

A planting of a few summers ago, in the south-facing border of the Eagle Court. The grey leaves of English lavender and glaucous euphorbia leaves provide a foil for yellow and blue flowers. The lavender flowers coincide with blue agapanthus to complement Argyranthemum *'Jamaica Primrose'.*

In snug beds at the base of the house wall, Algerian iris, *Iris unguicularis*, flowers in warm spells in winter, between clumps of *Corydalis lutea* and ceratostigma; small starry ipheons spread in the cracks between the stone flags. Climbing roses (the apricot 'Climbing Lady Hillingdon' and dark red scented 'Guinée'), intertwined with clematis (*Clematis viticella, C.v.* 'Purpurea Plena Elegans' and *C. campaniflora*) and *Schizophragma integrifolium* are all trained on the lower part of the façade.

Near the house, on the narrow terrace separated from the lawn and outer borders by a low wall, large Italian-style pots (made with reconstituted Ham stone but mellow and lichen-covered with age) are planted simply with regale lilies to flower towards the end of June. Other containers here are for seasonal displays; arrangements are changed at intervals through the summer and depend on back-up greenhouse work. On the steep steps leading down from the front door, in shade until early afternoon, there are pots of *Francoa sonchifolia*, the dark-flowered chocolate-scented *Cosmos atrosanguineus* and *Galactites* (thistles with elegant veined or variegated leaves). Twin pots against the wall contain hybrid bomareas trained to twine on bamboo canes. Kept in the greenhouse to get maximum heat until almost in flower, the green *Zinnia* 'Envy' is brought out for July and August. Below the wall a stiff ribbon edge of lavender (*Lavandula* 'Hidcote') is softened by self-seeding *Verbena bonariensis*, with flat mauve heads carried on tall square-shaped stems in August and September. Sprawling bushes of rosemary and seedlings of French lavender (*Lavandula stoechas*) frame the terrace and pathway.

Although in the Eagle Court, especially in April and May, the characteristic colours of spring prevail – particularly blues and yellows – none is pure and bright in hue. They are pale or darker hues which fade gently away into mauve and cream shades and tints. Except for some orange crown imperials (*Fritillaria imperialis*), supplied in error for the pale yellow form some twelve years ago, there are no colours from the warmer segment of the spectrum. Instead strong accents are provided by plant shapes and good foliage, which extend through all the seasons. Greens and greys and the shapes and densities they convey are most important in this garden. Pure undiluted primary colours seldom look effective placed together and I prefer to separate cool colours from the warmer hues. This is a part of my general garden philosophy which was acquired, I think, both by reading Gertrude Jekyll's books and from looking after Mrs Reiss's garden.

The blue and silver border at Royaumont contains many of the same colour elements as the Eagle Court. Blue caryopteris and salvias are united by silvery artemisias. Hydrangea arborescens *produces pale globular heads in late summer, above a carpet of hosta leaves.*

Box and Yew Topiary

THE CLASSIC mushroom-like domes of clipped box (*Buxus sempervirens*) at Tintinhull are a very simple sort of topiary – so simple and severe that to topiary fans intent on complicated fanciful shapes they probably seem quite dull. They are intended, however, not as decorative adjuncts but rather as a deliberate part of the garden design. Clipped and groomed immaculately, and as architectural as the old brick walls and gateways, they frame the pathway and control perspective.

Inspired at Bettiscombe by Tintinhull themes, I have used English yew to create similar rhythmic effects. Two avenues of eight yews each – one inside the walled garden, the other outside – are being trained as pyramids. Although now only 2m/7ft tall, they will develop to 4.5m/15ft in height with at least a 1.8m/6ft square base. Together with the existing walls and grass, they are the most important elements in the design of the garden, linking front and back into an integrated space.

Topiary, defined today as the art of shaping trees and shrubs by clipping and training, has a long history. The word derives from the Greek *topia* meaning landscapes, refined in the Latin *topiaria opera*, used by Pliny the Elder to indicate any kind of ornamental gardening; Pliny attributed the invention of tree-clipping to Matius at the end of the first century BC. References to the clipping and shaping of cypress, ivy and box in both Cicero's and Pliny the Younger's letters – the latter had his gardener's name outlined in box – indicate a strong interest in sculptural forms and definition in early gardening. Although little is recorded of any topiary practices in medieval Europe, there was a dramatic revival of interest from the fifteenth century on. In the famous Rucellai garden in Florence, created in the second half of the fifteenth century, evergreen shrubs were trained on withy (willow) frames into 'spheres, porticoes, temples, vases, urns, apes, donkeys, oxen, a bear, giants, men, women'. In the accounts for Hampton Court there exist bills for the withy materials on which plants – evergreen and deciduous – were trained. These date to the middle of the sixteenth century, and the resulting topiary is described by a visiting German in 1599.

In his essay 'Of Gardens' (1625) the eminent English philosopher and essayist Francis Bacon stated his preference for simple shapes such as 'little low hedges round like welts, with some pretty pyramids ... and in some places fair columns' – this in a century which saw almost every known small tree or shrub being ruthlessly tortured into elaborate, often frivolous, topiary shapes. At this period the 'ordering' of trees and shrubs into alleys and shapes was far more important – at least in the French and Dutch schools of gardening – than growing flowers. The inspiration for much modern topiary derives from shapes created in the seventeenth century.

For the edging to the beds in the Herb Garden at the New York Botanical Garden in the Bronx, I chose a hardy Japanese box cultivar, Buxus microphylla 'Winter Gem', which survives both harsh winter temperatures and hot summers. Clipped at intervals throughout the summer – in the heat of New York it grows fast – the knot retains its neat geometric shape.

Left: *We find that the simplest way to trim the box domes is to start by cutting a wide strip from the bottom to the top, to act as a marker. Tarpaulin sheets laid around the bush catch the clippings.*

Right: *Once the marking strip has been cut, it is fairly easy to trim neatly all around the bush. We only remove the young growth, usually about 5cm/2in, made since the previous year's annual trim. Clipping should be tightest around any gaps, as this will stimulate new growth.*

Like Francis Bacon, I prefer simple strung-out lines rather than whimsical features – perhaps because subconsciously I associate the more fanciful peacocks or rabbits with an alarming amount of fiddly work. I find the traditional evergreens such as box, yew, phillyrea and holly the best suited to topiary. I like topiary used as architecture and positively dislike shapes which have no relationship with house or garden. I admire topiary collections, as at Levens in Cumbria or Ladew in Maryland, and love the topiary kings and queens at Haseley Court in Oxfordshire.

Aspiring topiarists should remember the time element. The simplest sort of clipping, such as that of the Tintinhull domes, takes many years to develop to its required architectural form and scale. The domes, now 1.5m/5ft high and the same across at the bottom, have been there since the 1920s. They were almost certainly obtained already shaped and probably 60–75cm/2–2½ft in height; small bushes would have looked ridiculously out of scale with the house, brick walls and stone eagles. Nurseries for ready-made topiaries have probably existed whenever topiary has been fashionable. The famous topiary shapes in yew and box that once ornamented the garden at Compton Wynyates in Warwickshire were installed in 1895, a product of the late-Victorian cult of period revivalism, planted to convey an 'antique' atmosphere and link the Tudor house with its past. We know that the pieces were obtained ready-made, mainly from the nursery of the aptly named Herbert J. Cutbush of Highgate and from Joseph Cheal of Crawley, who also provided plants at Hever Castle for the labyrinth and golden chessmen in that contemporary garden.

Of course it is easiest, if expensive, to buy plants ready-trained from a specialist. But much of the pleasure of the effect lies in its creation: ideally, plants to be made into new topiary shapes should be obtained some years earlier and trained in a nursery situation. Rounded shapes are much easier to cut and control than those with right angles and square edges. Pyramids and battlements cut in a hedge need a fine degree of precision in cutting. The lines should be marked with strings first. For arches, spheres and niches and for the fanciful shapes – peacocks, hens, animals, chessmen – it is advisable to have frames on which the plants are trained. Light iron or willow are both suitable but, of course, the iron will last longer. In some cases the frame itself will be attractive during the formative years. For the most complicated shapes more than one plant will be necessary. Judiciously chosen young shoots are trained and tied to the frame; others are clipped back. Strong outward-growing shoots must be tied in at an early stage or may have to be removed altogether. The more the plant is cut the more natural 'breaks' will occur, with more than one young shoot taking the place of each one that is cut. Old-fashioned shears or good pruners and a small saw are better tools for topiary than machine-driven hedge-cutters, as many of the shoots must be cut off individually.

Once formed, topiary is not a lot of work but immaculate grooming is essential. Clipping of established shapes is of course much easier than clipping to make new ones. At Tintinhull the annual clipping, usually completed in June, is done by eye; over the years, however, not all eyes have judged accurately and some domes are more pudding-shaped than others. Perhaps, to ensure uniformity, we should make a standard portable frame in laths or willow which would fit exactly over each dome

the whole operation takes two days. In spring, as growth begins, the bushes are given an artificial fertilizer – an all-rounder with lots of nitrogen – and a top-dressing of compost. Apart from this no other attention is required – except, perhaps, after snow-falls, when it is important to knock the heavy snow off with some sort of light switch, or even with your hands.

One of the pleasures of topiary lies in the reflection of light from differently angled surfaces in sun and shadow. Then, in spring fresh green growth contrasts with the older darker green leaves; contrasts experienced again a few weeks after the annual cut. This is especially true of box and yew, which are pre-eminent for more detailed topiary, although forms of holly and phillyrea, recommended in 1629 by John Parkinson, can look particularly appropriate in a garden in a seventeenth-century style.

The trimming of the first dome has been completed and the bush looks very fresh and tidy. Within a week of clipping the leaves turn brown, but after another few weeks the bushes are beautiful again, with a rush of pale new foliage.

during clipping. We cut back all of the year's growth to keep the domes the same size, but if you need to reduce size or to correct any asymmetry you can be much more ruthless. If you want to encourage an increase in size you should clip twice during the summer, removing half the new growth each time. In climates with hotter summers, such as most areas of the United States, ordinary *Buxus sempervirens* puts on so much mounded growth that it is almost impossible to keep it as trim as we manage in the British Isles. In the famous boxwood gardens of Virginia mature box bushes are allowed to develop their own sprawling shapes.

After they have been cut our bushes are fed with a dried organic fertilizer, scattered by hand to make sure it reaches the base of each plant. There are sixteen box plants and

A Passion for Hellebores

Helleborus orientalis

Helleborus orientalis Ballard's Strain

On pages 46-7, left to right:
Helleborus orientalis
Helleborus foetidus
Helleborus argutifolius

HELLEBORES COULD become a grand passion. Their flowers – in most forms actually sepals – come in a wide range of muted colours: creamy-blushed purples, plum, pink, primrose-yellows, greens and mysterious blue-black, many with delicate spotting on the inside. Individually beautiful, their flowering in midwinter and spring makes them particularly precious and welcome. And they are not only flowerers. Their green foliage, deeply divided like the fingers of a hand and in some cases evergreen, is almost as desirable as the flowers and makes them attractive in the garden throughout the year.

Hellebores are generally good companion plants and, liking shade (although tolerant of sun), can be placed in corners where many other plants would not thrive – under the outer rims of the canopies of deciduous trees and shrubs, for example. Any ordinary well-drained fertile soil will do for most hellebores. All benefit from dressing with rich compost, and a dark mulch added just before flowering helps to set off the blooms as well as conditioning the soil and improving fertility. They do need periodic grooming: dead or blemished leaves should be removed in early spring, to show off the flowers at their best, and again in summer; the stems of the taller varieties, such as *Helleborus argutifolius* and *H. foetidus*, can be unobtrusively staked.

Most of us, unless already hellebore specialists, will start by growing those that are easiest and grow quickest; these include the Lenten hellebores (*H. orientalis* of gardens), the Corsican *H. argutifolius*, and the stinking hellebore, *H. foetidus*.

Everyone finds space for some of the Lenten hellebores, a range of hybrids based

Helleborus lividus

Helleborus orientalis

Helleborus torquatus 'Pluto'

Helleborus × sternii

on *H. orientalis* and often called simply Orientalis hybrids (botanically they are *H. × hybridus*). They are among the toughest of the group, well able to stand extremes of heat and cold. Their flowers are sculptured saucers in tints and shades between blush-white and plum, often spotted inside with crimson and maroon and subtly flushed with green. They seed freely, the seed germinating around the crown and sometimes under the leaves of a mature clump.

The Lenten hellebores look good with appropriate spring companions such as snowdrops, erythroniums, epimediums and wood anemones, which all enjoy the same conditions. For summer effects shade-tolerant lilies such as the Turk's cap lily (*Lilium martagon*) and toad lilies (*Tricyrtis formosana*) can be planted between the hellebore clumps.

I could not be without the Corsican species *Helleborus argutifolius* – as handsome as a shrub and growing to over 1m/3ft in height and spread, with bold spiny grey-green leaves and clusters of green-cupped flowers. Grow it with similar Mediterranean hillside plants: shrubby euphorbias, rosemary, lavenders, brooms and cistus. Its more tender relative

H. lividus can be a wonderful pot plant, but needs winter protection. The hybrid of these two species, *H. × sternii*, has a distinctive pink blush to the back of its leaves.

H. foetidus – native all over Europe with the best forms coming from the south – has narrow finely fingered leaves and cylindrically shaped small pale green flowers, each with a reddish band at the tip. Forms of it grow to 1.2m/4ft. It has a wilder appearance than other hellebores and will thrive and flower in any rough corner, but repays extra attention and sprucing up for a more visible flower bed.

I have never been charmed by the Christmas rose, *H. niger*, or any of its forms or hybrids. I do not want large white flowers, much preferring the grace and subtle interest of the green hellebores. I would like to have again some of the green-flowered subspecies of *H. multifidus*. Many years ago I treasured *H.m.* ssp. *bocconei* from central Italy. I recommend a collection of 'greens' in which I would include this, along with *H. viridis* – a British native – and forms of the sought-after *H. torquatus* from Serbia, with sepals dusky purple outside and green-coloured inside.

Euphorbias in the Garden

WITH THEIR handsome foliage and elegant habit, euphorbias or spurges are among the most diverse and useful of garden plants. The grandest are feature plants in their own right, while lower-growing species and hybrids play a humbler role, enhancing the effect of more striking neighbours. Some are shrubby plants, others perennial clump-formers or stoloniferous spreaders. Most prefer full sun and good drainage, thriving in Mediterranean conditions, but others, especially the wood spurge, *Euphorbia amygdaloides,* and its variants, enjoy dappled shade. All are tap-rooted and, grown from seed or cuttings, should be transplanted in their early stages before the roots become pot-bound – a common cause of failure.

Among the most handsome of the sun-lovers is the shrubby *E. characias.* This bold evergreen with narrow greyish leaves makes a graceful shape 1.2 m/4 ft high and across. It

Above: *Euphorbia characias* ssp. *wulfenii* 'John Tomlinson'

Right: *Euphorbia griffithii* 'Fireglow'

Below: *Euphorbia mellifera*

bears fine yellow flowers (or rather, strictly speaking, bracts) with deep brownish-purple centres for two months each spring. A short-lived species, it is a natural infiller, seeding between paving stones and in dry walls. The best forms are cultivars of *E.c. wulfenii*, such as 'Lambrook Gold' (originally found by Margery Fish in her garden at East Lambrook) and 'John Tomlinson'. The biennial stems produce clustered leaves in one year and flower spikes the next; the latter need cutting back as the flower head fades. Propagate these cultivars from cuttings of the young growth in spring or summer.

If you have a sheltered garden the tender *E. mellifera* from the Canary Islands deserves a place in full sun. Growing to 1.8m/6ft to make a rounded bush, it has beautiful velvet-textured veined green foliage and honey-scented pinkish-brown flower heads.

In contrast the evergreen species *E. myrsinites* from southern Europe and Asia Minor only grows to 20cm/8in; it has trailing stems with pointed glaucous fleshy leaves and, in early spring, bright lime-green terminal inflorescences, which assume a pinkish tint as they fade. This euphorbia likes very well-drained soil: grow it over a low wall or in a tub, perhaps beside blue-flowered *Scilla bifolia*, a plant of the same native habitat. Even more attractive is the taller *E. rigida* (*E. biglandulosa*), with spiralling leaves clasping the stems and bright yellow flowers.

From the eastern Himalaya comes *E. griffithii*: its cultivars *E.g.* 'Fireglow' and 'Dixter' have brick-red and orange flowers respectively, carried over greenish-orange foliage. Enjoying any good soil in sun or

part shade, the spreading roots quickly establish to make substantial groups. Another Asiatic spurge, *E. sikkimensis*, does best in moist soil. Its translucent red leaves with white veins are startling as they rise through the soil in spring; much later in the season flower heads on spaced willowy stems are flat and greenish-yellow. We grow it pushing through a blue pulmonaria.

Forms of the spring-flowering woodland spurge *E. amygdaloides* are more muted in appearance. They are companion plants rather than striking on their own. *E.a.* var. *robbiae*, an almost evergreen colonizer with broad darkest green rosettes and yellowish-green spring flowers, is an admirable groundcover plant to lighten a dark corner.

The small feathery *E. cyparissias*, although disappearing in winter, is another groundcover plant; however, it does not like to be shaded by overhead plants. It runs freely but if controlled is most appealing, making a carpet of lacy lime-green stems in early summer. Its woodland cousins *E. dulcis* and *E. stricta* are almost weeds but very desirable for their rich autumn colouring. Allowed to weave and seed around shrubs and perennials they make a fine cover for awkward areas of bare soil.

Right: *It is important to wear gloves, and to work with care, when deadheading the large woody euphorbias (varieties of* Euphorbia characias *and* E.c. ssp. wulfenii *cultivars), as the lactose glue which oozes out from a cut stem can produce a skin rash or damage the eyes. Leaving a few flowers – those which show least – to set seed, I cut off most of the long-stemmed flower heads as near to the base of the plant as I can reach.*

In the Middle Garden, running from sunlight into the shadow of the evergreen oaks and between the two outer borders with their casual planting, the central pathway and box domes play a major role in holding the design together. A view from the attic windows reveals the pattern of symmetrically arranged golden foliage plants in the Fountain Garden beyond.

A woodland garden
Drought-tolerant planting
Seasonal performance
Encouraging self-seeders
Anemones for spring and autumn
Elegant hydrangeas

THE MIDDLE GARDEN

MUCH LESS CAREFULLY arranged than the Eagle Court, the Middle Garden has a more natural 'woodland' style, with less obvious architectural planting and a less immediately identifiable colour scheme. But although planting seems haphazard, with single small specimen trees and shrubs of different heights, there is still essential balance and symmetry. The design is held together by some strong features, such as the repetition of the pattern of clipped domes of box flanking the axial stone pathway that continues to the western end of the garden. The taller bushy planting is linked on the horizontal level with massed groundcover. Except for the central pathway, all the horizontal patterns formed by grass and groundcover plants curve rather than making right-angled bends. Curving flower beds enfold a central lawn, the lawn panels becoming a well of light in the midst of thick planting. On the north side, a narrow grass pathway, framed by upright junipers, reveals the rectangular canal in the Pool Garden and allows access. The vista in reverse, from the Pool Garden summerhouse down the canal into the Middle Garden, is centred on a replica of an eighteenth-century urn, set on a plinth against the south wall.

The planting is dominated by two tall evergreen oaks (*Quercus ilex*) on the south-west corner. While creating a wide pocket of dense dry shade (their roots extend well beyond their overhead canopies), these leafy trees effectively screen noise and movement from the neighbouring village lane and, of course, frame the sky. Smaller trees combined with large shrubs accentuate the perimeter planting along the outer wall and make a division between the Middle Garden and the Fountain Garden to the west and the colourful Pool Garden on the north. Smaller shrubs, graceful mauve- and pink-flowered shrub roses and other woody plants, carry the garden through all the seasons, a plant theme allowing a certain amount of licence in replacement and improvement.

At first glance there may seem to be no distinctive scheme or guidelines; there are no strongly shaped plant blocks and the effects

achieved are pictorial rather than architectural: a composition of light and shade, openness and density, with touches of balancing colour, shades and hues dominated by pinks and mauves. Partly because there are fewer fixed rules, but also because each plant becomes part of the overall scheme rather than having much individual importance, we have found this area the easiest to restore to the character intended by Mrs Reiss. If we add new plants they are immediately integrated rather than remaining obvious additions. The point about this garden is that the framework, although firmly present, is unobtrusive. It is disguised by naturalness in planting. I find it sets a theme for a relaxed sort of planting which often proves more suitable for implementation in a client's garden than more formal hedged schemes or geometric patterns.

Natural planting, done by eye and whenever possible implemented on site rather than from a blueprint, is far more difficult than laying out formal patterns to a rule book. Much of my design work is superimposed on an existing garden layout; occasionally it has to be integrated into awkward sloping terrain with existing trees. Few clients want a garden even as formal as Tintinhull. American garden owners, especially, want a style that fits into their native, often thickly wooded, landscape. In a garden I designed in Austin, Texas, giant live oaks (*Quercus virginiana* – the American south's equivalent to the holm oak, *Quercus ilex*) are dominant features. Curving drives, pathways and beds are all related to the oak canopies which frame the sky and, with their roots, control the ground area which can reasonably be planted. Lawn walks alternately widen and narrow to make pools of light between the groves of dark oak; shrubs, undercarpeted with smaller plants, integrate a naturalistic pattern, very much in the same style as the Middle Garden at Tintinhull, though on a much larger scale.

Mrs Reiss also had clear-cut practical objectives, the most important of which was to ensure that this part of the garden would be screened from the adjacent Pool Garden by thick perimeter planting. She chose to do this with mixed shrubby planting, rather than by emphasizing the edges with a line of trees or hedging plants. Until 1947 the Pool Garden was a tennis court and this planting may have been left over from those days. A rigid row of screening trees or large shrubs would have drawn attention to a court and accentuated its straight netting. Mrs Reiss knew that thick planting of high and low shrubs mixed together would make a much more effective visual barrier.

A reproduction of the eighteenth-century Kent's Urn is framed by the flowers and leaves of the woodland plants along the south border in the Middle Garden. By late summer pink Japanese anemones, well established between hydrangeas, provide the main flowering interest in beds which in spring are carpeted with woodland anemones and erythroniums. Heathers supply winter colour.

Erythronium revolutum

Clematis × *jouiniana*

Erythronium dens-canis

SPRING PLANTING

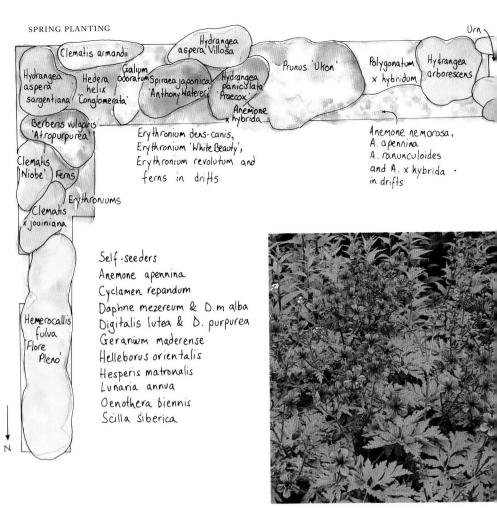

Clematis armandii

Hydrangea aspera Villosa

Prunus 'Ukon'

Polygonatum × hybridum

Hydrangea arborescens

Urn

Hydrangea aspera sargentiana

Hedera helix 'Conglomerata'

Galium odoratum

Spiraea japonica 'Anthony Waterer'

Hydrangea paniculata Praecox'

Anemone × hybrida

Berberis vulgaris 'Atropurpurea'

Erythronium dens-canis, Erythronium 'White Beauty', Erythronium revolutum and ferns in drifts

Anemone nemorosa, A. apennina A. ranunculoides and A. × hybrida in drifts

Clematis 'Niobe'

Ferns

Erythroniums

Clematis × jouiniana

Hemerocallis fulva 'Flore Pleno'

N

Self-seeders
Anemone apennina
Cyclamen repandum
Daphne mezereum & D. m alba
Digitalis lutea & D. purpurea
Geranium maderense
Helleborus orientalis
Hesperis matronalis
Lunaria annua
Oenothera biennis
Scilla siberica

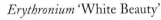

Geranium palmatum

Erythronium 'White Beauty'

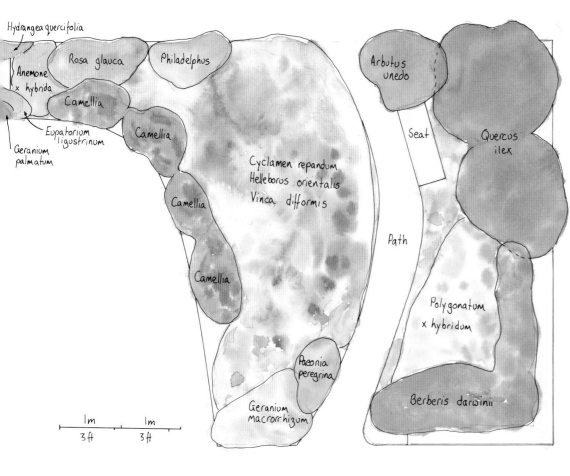

Hydrangea quercifolia

Rosa glauca

Philadelphus

Anemone × hybrida

Camellia

Eupatorium ligustrinum

Geranium palmatum

Camellia

Camellia

Cyclamen repandum
Helleborus orientalis
Vinca difformis

Arbutus unedo

Seat

Quercus ilex

Path

Camellia

Polygonatum × hybridum

Paeonia peregrina

Geranium macrorrhizum

Berberis darwinii

1m
___
3ft

1m
___
3ft

Arbutus unedo

Scilla siberica

Vinca difformis

Paeonia peregrina

Polygonatum × hybridum

Bupleurum fruticosum

Buglossoides purpurocaerulea

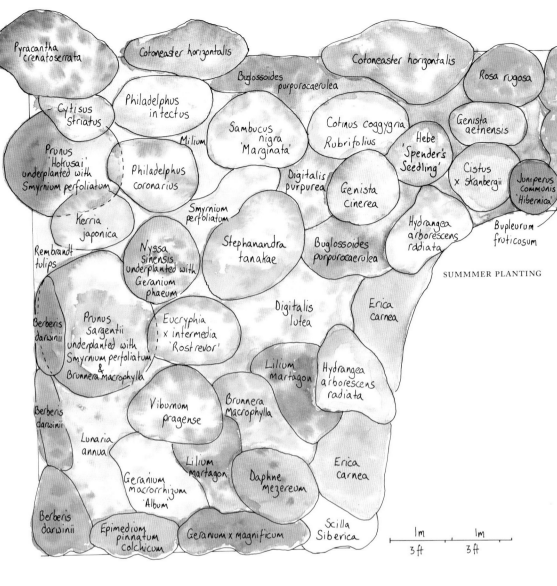

Pyracantha crenatoserrata

Cotoneaster horizontalis

Cotoneaster horizontalis

Buglossoides purpurocaerulea

Rosa rugosa

Cytisus striatus

Philadelphus intectus

Sambucus nigra 'Marginata'

Cotinus coggygria Rubrifolius

Hebe 'Spender's Seedling'

Genista aetnensis

Milium

Prunus 'Hokusai' underplanted with Smyrnium perfoliatum

Philadelphus coronarius

Digitalis purpurea

Genista cinerea

Cistus × skanbergii

Juniperus communis 'Hibernica'

Kerria japonica

Smyrnium perfoliatum

Hydrangea arborescens rdiata

Bupleurum fruticosum

Rembrandt tulips

Nyssa Sinensis underplanted with Geranium phaeum

Stephanandra tanakae

Buglossoides purpurocaerulea

SUMMMER PLANTING

Berberis darwinii

Prunus sargentii underplanted with Smyrnium perfoliatum & Brunnera macrophylla

Eucryphia × intermedia 'Rostrevor'

Digitalis lutea

Erica carnea

Berberis darwinii

Lilium martagon

Hydrangea arborescens radiata

Viburnum pragense

Brunnera Macrophylla

Lunaria annua

Lilium martagon

Erica carnea

Geranium macrorrhizum 'Album'

Daphne mezereum

Berberis darwinii

Epimedium pinnatum colchicum

Geranium × magnificum

Scilla Siberica

1m 1m
3ft 3ft

Lilium martagon

Daphne mezereum

Geranium × magnificum

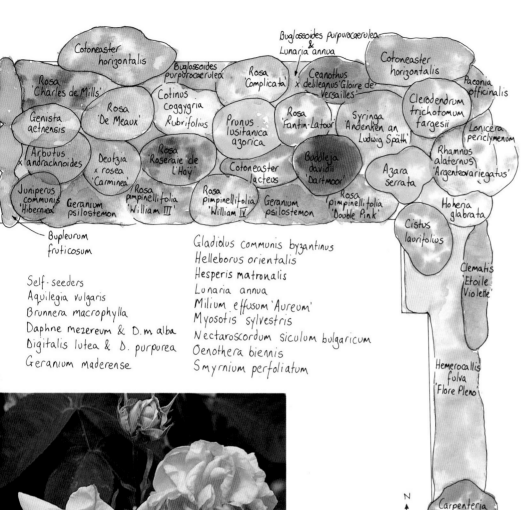

Cotoneaster horizontalis

Buglossoides purpurocaerulea & Lunaria annua

Rosa 'Charles de Mills'

Buglossoides purpurocaerulea

Rosa 'Complica'ta'

Ceanothus × delileanus 'Gloire de Versailles'

Cotoneaster horizontalis

Paeonia officinalis

Rosa 'De Meaux'

Cotinus coggygria Rubrifolius

Prunus lusitanica azorica

Rosa 'Fantin-Latour'

Syringa 'Andenken an Ludwig Späth'

Clerodendrum trichotomum fargesii

Lonicera periclymenum

Genista aetnensis

Arbutus × andrachnoides

Deutzia × rosea 'Carminea'

Rosa 'Roseraie de l'Haÿ'

Cotoneaster lacteus

Buddleja davidii 'Dartmoor'

Azara serrata

Rhamnus alaternus 'Argenteovariegatus'

Juniperus communis 'Hibernica'

Geranium psilostemon

Rosa pimpinellifolia 'William III'

Rosa pimpinellifolia 'William IV'

Geranium psilostemon

Rosa pimpinellifolia 'Double Pink'

Hoheria glabrata

Bupleurum fruticosum

Cistus laurifolius

Clematis 'Etoile Violette'

Hemerocallis fulva 'Flore Pleno'

N

Carpenteria californica

Self-seeders
Aquilegia vulgaris
Brunnera macrophylla
Daphne mezereum & D.m alba
Digitalis lutea & D. purpurea
Geranium maderense

Gladiolus communis byzantinus
Helleborus orientalis
Hesperis matronalis
Lunaria annua
Milium effusum 'Aureum'
Myosotis sylvestris
Nectaroscordum siculum bulgaricum
Oenothera biennis
Smyrnium perfoliatum

Azara serrata

Hoheria glabrata

Clematis 'Etoile Violette'

Rosa 'Fantin-Latour'

Rosa 'Roseraie de l'Haÿ'

Gladiolus communis ssp. *byzantinus* with *Geranium psilostemon*

THE MIDDLE GARDEN 57

Drought-tolerant Planting

A LTHOUGH AT TINTINHULL each compartment is linked by paths, carefully planned vistas and a repetition of planting, any individual section, when you are in it, remains almost totally hidden from adjacent areas. In 1980, our first summer at Tintinhull, it was four years after the severe drought of 1976. We found that many of the larger shrubs in the wide beds of the Middle Garden, those separating it from the Pool Garden to the north, had never fully recovered from the stress occasioned by lack of water and were gradually deteriorating. They no longer operated as a dense screen but left more open views and in many cases needed replacing. Our first task was, so far as possible, to save the old plants (this was achieved, to some extent, by hard pruning and feeding). We also wanted to introduce new shrubs – mainly bulky and evergreen with broad, rounded shapes rather than staccato verticals – to help provide a permanent and effective screen. With a projected pattern of hot summers to come, the intention was that these shrubs should be as drought-tolerant as possible, as well as being able to withstand freak cold winters.

We replaced much of the original planting and also added shrubs of our own choice. Among these, in the north-east bed in full sun, are Mediterranean-type evergreens, including a form of Portugal laurel from the Azores (*Prunus lusitanica* ssp. *azorica*) with golden-green foliage and the magnificent *Arbutus × andrachnoides* (a hybrid of the Greek *A. andrachne* and *A. unedo*), with peeling cinnamon-red bark. In a corner of this bed, sheltered from wind chill and turbulence, a tender evergreen, *Azara serrata* from Chile, with clusters of yellow stamen-like flowers in July, grows beside a replacement *Hoheria glabrata* from New Zealand, with cherry-like white blossom crowding the branches in the same month. Both will flower well in a year following a hot summer. Down the middle of the bed, part of a spine of taller shrubs, are an upright evergreen cotoneaster, the vigorous *Cotoneaster lacteus* we first admired as a tall hedge at Glasnevin in Dublin, with long-lasting clusters of red fruits, and the bushy *Rhamnus alaternus* 'Argenteovariegatus', its leaves marbled grey and cream. Bushes of the glaucous-leaved Mediterranean *Bupleurum fruticosum* now flank the pathway vista to the Pool Garden. This shrub needs an annual spring trim. It is a tedious task, to be done slowly with secateurs, but well worth the effort: the carefully sculpted rounded shapes look glorious in summer when the bushes produce their umbels of yellow flowers, turning to buff-gold as the seed ripens.

A gap in the screen of roses and evergreen and deciduous shrubs on the north side of the Middle Garden allows a glimpse through to the Pool Garden's central canal and the summerhouse.

Some large shrub roses, such as *Rosa* 'Complicata', *R.* 'Fantin-Latour' and the Rugosa 'Roseraie de l'Haÿ' grow between the shrubs, along with the Gallica 'Charles de Mills' and Centifolia 'De Meaux'. The smaller suckering Scotch burnet roses (varieties of *R. pimpinellifolia*) which do so well at Tintinhull – 'Double Pink', white 'William IV' and magenta-flowered 'William III' – thrive along the southern edge of the bed. A pretty pink deutzia (*Deutzia × rosea* 'Carminea'), quite modest in size when we came in 1980 but possibly planted by Mrs Reiss, has grown to make a 2m/7ft spread. *Buddleja davidii* 'Dartmoor', with purple-crimson flowers, strikes a dark note.

In the north-west bed there had been less drought damage and new shrubs grew quickly to complement old plantings which have survived and are still healthy after forty years or so. Among the latter

the more tender *O. armatus,* one of E.H. Wilson's introductions, with thick leaves edged with spiny teeth, very like a large holly, which flowers as summer ends. Although these osmanthus all come from the Far East, none of them looks at all exotic. These would be a start, together with *Phillyrea latifolia,* one of the finest small trees from the Mediterranean basin, with flickering finely toothed leaves, translucent when young, and a broad canopy. I have seen it in groves in its native habitat and it is spectacular at Hatfield House in Hertfordshire, where it grows along the courtyard balustrading. There are also exotic hollies, again from the Far East, among them *Ilex fargesii* and *I. latifolia.*

Along the northern edge of the Middle Garden are Mrs Reiss's fans of herringbone cotoneaster (*Cotoneaster horizontalis*), pruned to cascade and spread over the path beneath, with glorious autumn foliage and berries, one of her most successful ideas. Some people might scorn the use of such an ordinary plant in an important situation but it seems just right to me; I like to use it in my designs, draped against balustrading or a low wall. *C. microphyllus,* with smaller habit and leaves, can be used in a similar way.

The use of groundcover plants in this area is classical: both evergreen and deciduous shrubs make a layer of planting under the limbs of the small trees, while low-growing plants – shrubs and perennials – cover the ground and keep it moist in summer and suppress weed germination. Bulbs come mainly in spring, and other taller summer-flowering perennials and biennials find just enough bare earth to survive and flower beside denser carpeting plants.

Under the north-facing wall along the lane spring bulbs provide the predominant groundcover. Scillas and anemones, cyclamen and erythroniums are succeeded by scented woodruff (*Galium odoratum*). In the middle beds there are more perennials, especially blue-flowered *Buglossoides purpurocaerulea,* intermixed with other blues such as self-seeding forget-me-nots and *Brunnera macrophylla.* In the shadiest part in the north-west bed there are crane's-bill geraniums and, encouraged by us, self-seeding *Smyrnium perfoliatum* with lime-yellow bracts in spring. All of these knit together to make an effective barrier against weed germination.

The old favourite daylily *Hemerocallis fulva* 'Flore Pleno' is massed under the west-facing 'Eagle' walls, its young golden foliage emerging in late winter. *Cyclamen repandum,* Solomon's seal (*Polygonatum × hybridum*), Lenten hellebores and the white-starred winter-flowering periwinkle *Vinca difformis,* now mixed with a self-made blue form, spread happily in the dry soil under the deep shade of the evergreen oaks, where little else would flourish.

Throughout the whole of the Middle Garden, wherever there is space among the drifts of groundcovers, scented mauve and white mezereums (*Daphne mezereum* and *D.m.* f. *alba*) and sweet rocket are encouraged to seed casually, alongside many biennials such as evening primrose, honesty, foxgloves and *Geranium maderense.*

are broad-headed spring-flowering cherries, backed by a tough *Pyracantha crenatoserrata* that produces clouds of white in early summer, a tall variegated elder (*Sambucus nigra* 'Marginata') and a neighbouring philadelphus (*Philadelphus intectus*) which grows to 4m/13ft. The most successful additions have been a tough evergreen viburnum from Prague (*Viburnum* 'Pragense'), lime-tolerant *Eucryphia × intermedia* 'Rostrevor', brown-stemmed *Stephanandra tanakae* and a scattering of shrub roses.

If space permitted or if I were making a similar new bed I would probably use some more of my favourite evergreen shrubs for their foliage and general appearance. These were among my greatest interests when I was gardening at Hadspen House (also in Somerset), in the 1970s. I particularly enjoy the different Asiatic holly-like osmanthus, especially *Osmanthus heterophyllus* (including the variegated varieties), small-leaved *O. delavayi* (for its deliciously scented spring flowers) and dome-shaped dark-leaved *O. decorus.* All of these are hardy. I used to grow two Chinese species at Hadspen: *O. yunnanensis,* a fast-growing small tree or large shrub with olive-green leaves and tiny fragrant white flowers in late winter, and

Seasonal Performance

In a mild spell in January the white periwinkle starts to perform under the tall evergreen oaks. During the next two months seedling hellebores followed by the sweetly fragrant carmine-flowered *Cyclamen repandum* emerge through the periwinkle foliage, both plants continually colonizing any neighbouring pockets of bare earth under shrubs. Mrs Reiss had camellias here but these, suffering from neglect, were removed, to be replaced with unnamed red camellias taken as cuttings from a friend's garden in Italy. The original planting scheme, before the roots of the oaks had spread so far, also included some small rhododendrons, but these have succumbed to drought. The soil at Tintinhull is almost neutral, but conditions do not really suit ericaceous plants, and even the camellias require frequent doses of sequestrene.

By March spears of Solomon's seal appear nearer the boles of the trees. The evergreen *Berberis darwinii* from South America, planted as a hedge between the Middle Garden and the Fountain Garden, also flowers early, its yellow blooms replaced in midsummer with glowing turquoise fruits. The cherries, as planned by Phyllis Reiss, flower in an organized succession. Round-headed Sargent's cherry, *Prunus sargentii*, also renowned for the splendid autumn foliage effects rare in cherries, opens the season with single pink flowers; *P.* 'Hokusai' has large semi-double flowers a little later, and a more spreading habit. Beside the wall *P.* 'Ukon' is taller, with yellowish-green flowers. This tree and the specimen in Eagle Court have been badly damaged by birds who attack dormant buds in winter, leaving long straggly limbs without flower or leaf, and they should soon be replaced. Evergreen *Clematis armandii* clambers over the wall and into neighbouring shrubs, scenting the spring garden with its fragrant white flowers; it needs cutting back after flowering, a task easily neglected in the busiest time of early summer.

Under the wall native wood anemones (*Anemone nemorosa*) are massed to produce a spring carpet of white and green, while the ground-hugging yellow-flowered *A. ranunculoides* yearly increases its spread and escaped seedlings – distributed by birds – of blue-flowered *A. apennina* appear everywhere. *Cyclamen repandum* seeds freely here among clumps of Solomon's seal and crowns of creeping scented woodruff. This 'natural' planting is given more formality with blocks of erythroniums, their shining leaves making focal points even before the flowers open their nodding heads in late spring. We grow white *Erythronium* 'White Beauty' and the yellow form of the species, *E. revolutum* from Californian woodlands, as

well as *E. dens-canis,* the native European dog's-tooth violet, known as the trout or fawn lily in the United States, and much loved for its glaucous spotted leaves and violet-pink swept-back flower petals. Corms need time to establish and should be left undisturbed. As flowering ends the leaves begin to die down and by midsummer they are cleared away to leave an empty space in the garden scheme. I have found that ferns, which emerge relatively late in spring, can be grown successively between the erythronium corms without inhibiting their vigour.

In the north-west bed a kerria – the single-flowered *Kerria japonica* – and a tall *Genista cinerea* flower early. Both survive well in this dry area, as does the interesting *Smyrnium perfoliatum* from central Asia. Beneath are three shade-tolerant groundhuggers, all members of the Boraginaceae family. *Brunnera macrophylla*, with forget-me-not-like flowers, rapidly increases by annual self-seeding. *Buglossoides purpurocaerulea* has arching tip-rooting stems, capable of colonizing any area very rapidly. These two combine with ordinary biennial forget-me-nots to make swirling blue patterns under the yellow-flowered shrubs and the smyrniums with their acid-yellow bracts. The smyrniums and forget-me-nots are pulled out as soon as the seed is ripe and dispersed. The long questing fronds of the buglossoides (perhaps still more easily recognized by its old name of lithospermum) need cutting back by mid- to late summer or they will almost strangle some of the plants. In a small garden – or even here – the less vigorous form of brunnera, *Brunnera macrophylla* 'Hadspen Cream', with leaves delicately splashed with white, could be an alternative, or the more elegant and slightly earlier-flowering *Pulmonaria angustifolia*, or a bugle, *Ajuga reptans*.

In early summer, in the north-east bed, the tall old lilac (*Syringa vulgaris* 'Andenken an Ludwig Späth') chosen by Mrs Reiss has dark violet flowers and twiggy burnet roses have pink, white and magenta clustered flowers. By full summer mauve and pale pink shrub roses with scented white-flowered philadelphus and the one floriferous pink deutzia dominate the main beds. Crane's-bill geraniums make good companions, their mainly pale colouring matching the gentle hues of the roses. They have a long flowering season and stretch back in drifts under the shade of the earlier-flowering cherries and towards the big evergreen oaks. The most striking is the tall *Geranium psilostemon*, with magenta petals and a black eye, sited in full sun. All of these hardy geraniums have to be cut back to the ground after flowering; they will then produce fresh new foliage to

Above left: *The scented flowers of* Cyclamen repandum *are pinkish-carmine. Reputedly tender, it thrives at Tintinhull.*

Above right: *The native wood anemone* (Anemone nemorosa) *flowers with* Cyclamen repandum *in the shaded south border.*

improve the beds' late-summer appearance, and occasionally some more flowers as well.

Throughout this area colour schemes are seasonal, almost monthly 'episodes' rather than all-over themes; spring yellows precede dark purples and pinks, then come swathes of blue ground carpeting, then pinks and mysterious purples from old roses, followed by the dark-flowered *Buddleja davidii* 'Dartmoor' and pink- and white-flowered hydrangeas. I really prefer this sort of colour planning to the more self-conscious arrangements in other Tintinhull beds. I enjoy the monthly variations.

Some of the roses flower again, if briefly, but during the rest of the summer and autumn most of the flower and leaf interest of the central beds is located on the northern side, facing the Pool Garden. This show accompanies the main peak of the Pool Garden borders,

which is in July and August, and is more strictly colour orientated. In the north-west bed the golden Mount Etna broom (*Genista aetnensis*) is startling near a purple-bronze-leaved smoke bush (*Cotinus coggygria* Rubrifolius Group); pale evening primroses (*Oenothera biennis*) glow at dusk to link the colour scheme with the red and yellow border in the Pool Garden. The blue-flowered deciduous *Ceanothus × delileanus* 'Gloire de Versailles' correspondingly links the north-east bed with the pale-coloured Pool border. A new *Clerodendrum trichotomum* var. *fargesii* has fragrant white flowers enclosed in maroon-purple calyces. Later the flowers become turquoise-blue berries, still surrounded by the colourful calyces, resplendent for the autumn scene.

Along the outer wall bed, hydrangeas are grouped together in the light shade to give a solid impact as they flower in late summer above the ferns, Solomon's seal and ground-hugging scented woodruff. They include *Hydrangea aspera* Villosa Group, *H. arborescens*, *H. paniculata* 'Praecox', *H. quercifolia* and the velvet-leaved *H. aspera* ssp. *sargentiana*. The most drought-tolerant and most effective in flower is *H.a.* Villosa Group, but its new growth and flower buds are especially vulnerable to late spring frosts. At Tintinhull a young plant needs protecting in its first seasons.

Encouraging Self-seeders

Aquilegia vulgaris with *Rosa* 'Rosemary Rose'

Gladiolus communis ssp. *byzantinus*

I FIND THAT a practical approach to managing mixed borders, in which every iota of soil should be covered by plants, is to encourage proliferation of self-sown seedlings. They will extend the theme adopted for any one area, fill every empty space and, allowed to flower in season where they germinate, give the attractive and seemingly unplanned natural look that I am always seeking.

At Tintinhull we use this self-seeding method throughout the garden, in the formal colour borders as well as in the more natural-style beds in the Middle Garden. We do, however, limit the numbers of different plants in each area, believing that it is more effective to have an abundance of any one kind rather than just a few examples of a great variety. In most areas we have distinctive, easily recognizable colour schemes, so the seeders are chosen to augment and enrich these schemes.

This method of gardening fits perfectly into my garden philosophy. It sounds labour-saving and up to a point it is, but I have not adopted it to save time or work; it is done for effect. It does require a certain amount of skill and effort, particularly in weeding, for, to the uninitiated, many of these young seedlings look just like weeds. Maintenance depends on an observant eye and a controlling hand, or the garden will look a mess by midsummer and deteriorate even more in the following months.

Instead of being trimmed back in an orderly manner after flowering, as part of normal garden routine, at least a proportion of the desirable seeders must be allowed to set and disperse seed as flowering finishes. It is sufficient to keep just a few specimens of each plant for this purpose; you can also, of course, gather and scatter the seed. If space permits, the well-organized gardener can even grow examples of self-seeders in a nursery area, allowing them to set seed there, then gathering it and scattering it where required.

I like to have strong woody plants in all borders: these establish a skeleton structure. They are placed with great care, their architectural role and contribution to the whole scheme without question. Around them are arranged the more permanent perennials. In the main borders at Tintinhull shrubs and perennials occupy 90 per cent of the space. In the Middle Garden and other more natural-looking areas there are more shrubs but perennials have less emphasis. Instead, self-seeding biennials and annuals play a major role. As the shrubs become established, probably in the second year after planning a scheme, other plants – mainly biennials and annuals but also some perennials – are encouraged to seed, to fill in the background around the shrub shapes. Unlike quick-growing bedding annuals, designed for massed effects in full sun, most of these plants do not need a richly prepared soil, but will look after themselves and flourish in poor conditions. They germinate wherever there is light and space. They colonize unlikely corners and spread in dappled shade. Though their beauty is often fleeting, they give an established air to a garden.

In all areas I use both tall plants and those which have more of a groundcover weed-suppressing role. In light shade smyrniums, foxgloves, evening primroses and lythrums give the required height; in sun verbascums, opium poppies, silver thistles, Miss Willmott's ghost and

Forget-me-nots in the Kitchen Garden

Nigella damascena 'Miss Jekyll'

Papaver somniferum

Viola 'Bowles' Black'

silybums are encouraged to seed and then selectively weeded out to achieve the look I want. In the Middle Garden we leave all the grannies' bonnets (*Aquilegia vulgaris*) in their different blues, while both here and in the Kitchen Garden ordinary forget-me-nots make a sea of blue in spring wherever space allows. Also in the Middle Garden are mauve-flowered Byzantine gladiolus and *Nectaroscordum siculum* ssp. *bulgaricum*, with nodding pinkish-green flowers; both are prolific seeders and seeds are probably moved around by mice or ants. In the Cedar Court we have encouraged the brightest blue love-in-a-mist, *Nigella damascena* 'Miss Jekyll', to seed itself between the rhizomes of the German flag irises. It makes a froth of intense colour above finely cut green leaves when the iris flowering is over. In the Kitchen Garden biennial sweet rocket (*Hesperis matronalis*) scatters its seeds behind clumps of summer roses. Among other prolific self-seeders at Tintinhull are violas (we have *Viola* 'Bowles' Black' in the Kitchen Garden); flaxes, including the annual scarlet *Linum grandiflorum* that we grow for pots around the pool; and poppies – the opium poppy, *Papaver somniferum*, the Welsh poppy, *Meconopsis cambrica* (which needs to be strictly controlled) and two horned poppies, *Glaucium corniculatum*, with scarlet flowers, and *G. flavum*, with clear yellow petals. Our rather special self-seeders include the unusual apricot-coloured *Collomia grandiflora*, which we have in the pale borders.

There are also always new plants to be tried. By taking advantage of self-seeders an established bed can readily be given a fresh look, a new lease of life, without changing the main feature plants.

Anemone coronaria St Brigid Group

Anemones for Spring and Autumn

G ARDEN ANEMONES fall into quite distinct categories, with very different garden effects. The genus is divided between those which have tubers or rhizomes and flower in spring, and those with a fibrous rootstock, which flower in late summer and can be part of main border schemes. The spring flowerers require a well-drained humus-rich soil and tolerate dry conditions during summer dormancy. The tall autumn flowerers need adequate moisture during their growing season through the summer.

Most familiar are the different species of spring anemone and the wind flowers or poppy anemones (*Anemone coronaria* hybrids). The spring anemones are shade-tolerant small naturalizers, mainly from Europe and the Middle East. Given a few years to establish, they will spread in drifts of colour under deciduous trees and shrubs and between snowdrops, hellebores, dog's-tooth violets and other shade-loving woodlanders such as creeping phlox from North America and the evergreen spurge, *Euphorbia amygdaloides* var. *robbiae*. The British native white wood anemone, *A. nemorosa*, is a great colonizer. It has many beautiful forms, among them *A.n.* 'Vestal', a double white, and *A.n.* 'Allenii', with pale lavender blooms. *A. ranunculoides* is similar, but lower-growing and with small yellow flowers. *A. apennina*, from Italy, south-eastern Europe and the eastern end of the Mediterranean, remains my favourite. A little taller than the earlier-flowering *A. blanda*, but otherwise very similar, it has deeply dissected fern-like leaves and erect stems carrying wide blue or white – occasionally pink – flowers, which turn towards the sun. At Tintinhull, with beds cultivated intensively for more than half a century, both the blue Apennine anemone and the white-flowered wood anemone have naturalized freely, the seeds of *A. apennina* distributed by birds to all parts of the garden, while *A. nemorosa* and its yellow cousin, *A. ranunculoides*, appear to increase only by their creeping rhizomes. Seed is set and the leaves die down soon after flowering. Here, with so many, we can afford to ignore them during the rest of the year, but in a new garden their positions should be clearly marked.

The *A. coronaria* hybrids, the type itself traditionally introduced to England in sacred soil by Crusaders from the Holy Land, are sun-lovers and mainly seen as the popular double-flowered St Brigid and single De Caen florists' flowers. More tender, the bulbs can be protected, or planted at any time in spring to give a display a few months later. The related hybrid *A. × fulgens* is the most brilliant of all scarlet flowers, the black centres outlined in yellow. The pasque flower (*Pulsatilla vulgaris*), with ferny foliage, a close anemone cousin, is another sun-lover.

The autumn-flowering anemones, often given the all-embracing title of Japanese anemones but actually including many from China, are usually forms of *Anemone × hybrida*, *A. vitifolia*, or the earlier species *A. hupehensis* from China (which will tolerate more summer heat and drought). Introduced after 1844, they can all be invasive but are strangely difficult to get established or even to move as mature plants. With broad maple- or vine-like rough leaves, which make them attractive throughout the growing season, these perennials contribute washes of white or pink to border effects through the last weeks of summer and are the flowering backdrop to many autumn borders. There are many good garden forms, all with wide segmented flowers and golden centres. *A. hupehensis* 'Hadspen Abundance' has rich pink almost double flowers, *A. h.* var.

Anemone × hybrida 'Honorine Jobert'

japonica 'Prinz Heinrich' is clear pink, *A. × hybrida* 'Queen Charlotte' single and paler. The star is *A. × h.* 'Honorine Jobert', a ghostly white with tall stems rising above dark foliage. Although tolerant of light shade, most of these anemones, even if originally placed at the back of a border, will gradually push forward towards a sunnier site; they are best allowed to thrive where they will. They should be given a thick mulch during the winter months and if they have to be moved must not be allowed to dry out before replanting. Unlike many other late performers, they need no staking.

On page 66, above: *Anemone blanda*
On page 66, below: *Anemone coronaria*
On page 67: *Anemone nemorosa* 'Allenii'

Anemone apennina

Elegant Hydrangeas

Hydrangea quercifolia

Hydrangeas are woodland plants and they look 'right' when grown in dappled shade in naturalistic gardens. As a total contrast, they have an architectural role. A pair can frame a gateway or define a vista, or a single specimen can be treated as a focal point. They also make marvellous container plants, especially for town gardens. Invaluable for their late-summer flowers, they continue to look good all winter, the flower heads generally deepening in colour with maturity and remaining decorative throughout the cold months until pruning time in spring. As an added bonus, most hydrangea flowers are well suited to drying for indoor arrangements.

With hydrangeas, success depends on wise pruning. Most flower on the previous year's growth. In early spring the stems that flowered last year are cut right to the ground, but as a general rule young shoots should not be touched (although if a bush has become very thick it may be best to remove some of the weakest of the new stems). After pruning the plant should be fed generously with an organic fertilizer to stimulate basal growth for next year's flowers. A few, including *Hydrangea paniculata* and *H. arborescens*, which flower at the tip of the current year's growth, can be treated more ruthlessly. With these, cut back the previous season's wood in late spring.

Although hydrangeas thrive more naturally in an acid loam, so long as they are well cared for and well fed most will tolerate akalinity or even chalk. However, I have to say that I covet the incredibly vivid wash of blue produced by mop-headed hortensia hydrangeas growing in rich acidic loam. Flowers achieve the deepest blue tones in a soil of pH 4.5 to 5.5. In limy soil the colour of the sterile florets becomes a muddy blueish-pink. If, like me, you garden on neutral or alkaline soil it is well worth considering growing the blue forms in containers with a specially prepared mix of acidic soil, or soil that has been treated with a blueing compound of aluminium sulphate.

The macrophyllas and serratas are the most domesticated of the hydrangeas. They are all clump-forming, producing new shoots from the base each season. Others suitable for smaller gardens are *H.* 'Ayesha' (of macrophylla origins) and *H. involucrata* 'Hortensis'. The larger hydrangeas, forms of *H. paniculata* (including 'Grandiflora' and 'Praecox' and the lovely new cultivar 'Kyushu'), and summer-flowering grandees such as the velvet-leaved *H. aspera* ssp. *sargentiana* and *H. heteromalla* Bretschneideri Group look their best in a woodland situation.

At Tintinhull we do well with *H. arborescens*, a medium-sized shrub with slender pointed leaves which bears its round mops of greenish-white sterile flowers from mid- to late summer. *H. aspera* Villosa Group also is nearly always a success, although a late spring frost can badly damage new growth. The colour of its large inflorescences is pink at Tintinhull but in more acid soil it is lilac-blue.

The tender Chinese *H. aspera* ssp. *sargentiana* is a noble shrub valuable for its foliage effects, as is the hardy American *H. quercifolia*, the oak-leaved hydrangea, with leaves which colour crimson in autumn. *H. aspera* ssp. *sargentiana* is augmented by large blueish (even in our soil) inflorescences in summer, while the oak-leaved hydrangea has sterile conical pinkish flowers, produced on last year's wood, so it will not flower in a cold climate. It can be trained as a wall shrub, and usually flowers and colours up well when it has the extra protection offered by a wall.

We grow all of these hydrangeas in the north-facing border in the Middle Garden, our nearest approach to a woodland situation, where wood and Apennine anemones, self-seeded *Cyclamen repandum* and clumps of erythroniums fill in the groundwork in spring. When in flower the hydrangeas are accompanied by drifts of pink Japanese anemones.

There are also climbing hydrangeas. Among the most popular, and deservedly so, is the self-clinging *H. anomala* ssp. *petiolaris*, which will climb to 20m/70ft along and up a shady wall, or can be encouraged to trail over a bank. With greenish-white lacecap flower corymbs, it is a slow starter but vigorous enough later. The tender evergreen *H. seemannii* has leathery leaves and creamy-white flower panicles. The related *Pileostegia viburnoides* and *Schizophragma hydrangeoides* – both members of the Hydrangeaceae – are also desirable for north-facing or shady walls. These two are self-clingers but can be guided when young. They both need some spring protection in their early years but are completely hardy as they mature.

Hydrangea aspera Villosa Group

Hydrangea anomala ssp. *petiolaris*

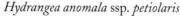

Hydrangea macrophylla 'Générale Vicomtesse de Vibraye'

Schizophragma hydrangeoides 'Roseum'

The view back to the house from the white seat at the end of the Fountain Garden. Tall yew hedges, spiky iris, white roses, the double avenue of box and the larger trees frame the façade. The layers of planting on different planes are integrated in a way that is typical of Tintinhull.

Gardens within gardens
A golden scheme
A white garden
A foliage garden
Caring for grey and silver plants
The distinguished dogwood family
Different daisies

THE FOUNTAIN GARDEN

I LOVE THE IDEA of a one-colour garden. Blue gardens, yellow gardens, pink and purple gardens are all attainable as extensions of other existing schemes. Only white gardens and hot-coloured gardens need to be set aside, hidden and framed by screens of hedges to come as a complete visual and emotional surprise. The white garden has a special charm at the end of the day, with whites and pastels glowing in the evening light, while reds and dark violets fade to nothing as dusk falls. Heavily scented white and cream flowers, or flowers with petals of the palest tints, set among greys, silvers and greens … it seems an entrancing dream.

At Tintinhull an enclosed white area forms the central feature of the Fountain Garden, the garden 'room' at the end of the axial walk. While each of the other 'rooms' at Tintinhull has a single theme, the Fountain Garden is subdivided by free-standing yew hedges (about 2m/7ft high) into a geometric complex of very small gardens, each with a separate plant or colour theme, arranged more or less as a square around the central white garden. In front of and behind the hedges are symmetrically laid out paths and beds, with different plant emphases depending on aspect. Some beds are in deep shade, others receive sun for most or part of the day. The whole area, at the

farthest western point of the garden, is also enclosed on two sides by the south and west perimeter walls, at the base of which is space for more flower beds.

The view from the Middle Garden takes your eye through two beds with a golden colour scheme, across the white garden with its central pool, and through openings in the yew, to terminate at an arbour of bay laurel sheltering an inviting white seat under the west wall. The bay laurel, clipped in an archway above the seat, is repeated as large, dense blocks (two cubes 3m/10ft × 1.2m/4ft × 1.2m/4ft) against the wall on either side. The seat looks east towards the main classical façade of the house, a view narrowed by foreground wings of yew, a pair of giant dogwoods with variegated leaves and, in season, statuesque silver Scotch thistles. In the distance the domes of box line the path below the tall eagles and frame the front door and steps.

The seat also allows a resting place in an intimate garden area, an area hidden from view until entered, and entirely devoted to the foliage effects of trees such as the dogwoods and lower-growing shrubs and perennials. A shady border around the back of the yew, under the south wall, also has a distinctive planting scheme. But it is the overall arrangement, and its relationship to the main axial path and the adjacent Kitchen Garden, which is of fundamental importance to the design. As in the rest of the garden, Mrs Reiss carefully planned vistas, entrances and exits to provide moments of surprise and satisfaction. She probably did it not with an elaborate scaled drawing but with bamboo canes and string – much the most satisfactory method if you can be on the spot.

From the central pool another view between the yew hedges opens to the north and carries the eye up the middle path of the Kitchen Garden to a typical Somerset cider orchard reached by a gate at the farthest end, a distance of some 45m/150ft. This is the only outside vista at Tintinhull. Even so the orchard is really an extension of the ornamental garden, rather than true countryside. Sheep are occasionally allowed in to graze beneath the trees. They give a delightful rural effect.

Two tall crab apples, *Malus* 'John Downie', flank the exit to the Kitchen Garden. This is perhaps the best-fruiting variety of all the crabs, with symmetrical heads bearing white blossom in spring and golden fruit in late summer. In spring daffodils line the central pathway of the vista through the Kitchen Garden and by June giant catmint overflows the edges. Opposite this entrance the garden ends at the perimeter wall on the south, where another pair of crabs, *Malus tschonoskii*, frames a shrub, the oak-leaved *Hydrangea quercifolia*. With white flower trusses, tinged slightly pink, and superb autumn foliage in a range of yellow, purple and scarlet, the hydrangea thoroughly earns its keep in this important position. Besides contributing to the formal planting scheme, the crabs are intended to screen activities across the public road.

Opposite: *In the two foliage beds at the west end of the garden, the two dominant giant dogwoods (Cornus controversa 'Variegata') rise above the rounded shapes of phlomis and brachyglottis and the leaves of the lower-growing hostas. White annual honesty (Lunaria annua alba) has seeded to give a spring display that complements the blue forget-me-nots.*

Above: *Looking north, beyond the silvery standard willows, the yew wings and the 'John Downie' crab apples, and through the hedges of catmint which stretch towards the cider orchard at the far end of the Kitchen Garden.*

THE FOUNTAIN GARDEN 73

A Golden Scheme

Yew hedge

Lilium Golden Splendor

Tanacetum parthenium 'Aureum'
Anemone apennina
& Anemone 'Honorine Jobert'

Lysimachia nummularia 'Aurea'

Lamium maculatum 'Aureum'

Philadelphus coronarius Variegatus

Tanacetum parthenium 'Aureum'

Philadelphus coronarius 'Aureus'

Philadelphus coronarius 'Aureus'

Physocarpus opulifolius 'Luteus'

Philadelphus coronarius 'Aureus'

Philadelphus coronarius 'Aureus'

Lonicera japonica 'Aureoreticulata' (clipped)

Hosta ventricosa

Lilium martagon, Scilla siberica & Meconopsis cambrica

Hosta sieboldiana 'Frances Williams'

THE FIRST SECTION of the Fountain Garden, immediately next to the Middle Garden, is reached by descending shallow central steps, an extension of the axial stone pathway, under the overhanging branches of the evergreen oaks. The levels on either side are adjusted by low stone walls, fringed with the hedge of *Berberis darwinii*, which helps to give a feeling of separateness. Still known as the azalea beds, this completely shaded area is divided into two

In the azalea beds golden-leaved Philadelphus coronarius *'Aureus' and a lingering* Rhododendron luteum *are undercarpeted with a medley of feverfew (*Tanacetum parthenium *'Aureum'), anemones, autumn-flowering colchicums, spring cyclamen (*Cyclamen repandum*) and self-seeded white honesty. By midsummer the leaves of most of the golden-foliaged plants become a more solemn green.*

Self seeders
Anemone apennina
Meconopsis cambrica
Scilla siberica
Tanacetum parthenium 'Aureum'

Philadelphus coronarius 'Aureus'

Meconopsis cambrica

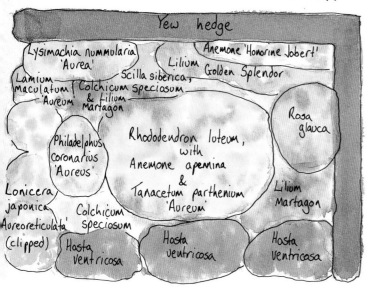

Yew hedge

Lysimachia nummularia 'Aurea'

Anemone 'Honorine Jobert'

Lilium Golden Splendor

Lamium maculatum 'Aureum'

Scilla siberica; Colchicum speciosum & Lilium Martagon

Philadelphus coronarius 'Aureus'

Rhododendron luteum, with Anemone apenina & Tanacetum parthenium 'Aureum'

Rosa glauca

Lonicera japonica Aureoreticulata (clipped)

Colchicum speciosum

Lilium Martagon

Hosta ventricosa

Hosta ventricosa

Hosta ventricosa

Lonicera japonica 'Aureoreticulata'

Lilium Golden Splendor

Scilla siberica

squares, with tall yew hedges providing a background to yellow and white scented flowers and plants with golden leaves. Originally the two beds were planted by Phyllis Reiss with the fragrant *Rhododendron luteum*, the well-known yellow species (then still known as *Azalea pontica*), underplanted with blue *Scilla siberica*. Today, although a few azaleas remain, the soil is too dry for them to thrive – the roots of the oaks penetrate deeply into these beds, soaking up all moisture – so we have extended and partly replaced the original theme with golden-leaved forms of various plants, both shrubby and herbaceous, all of which enjoy shade. In spring the beds are mulched heavily with organic compost to keep in as much moisture as possible. The scillas, increasing annually, are backed up by drifts of slightly later-flowering Apennine anemones, the blues complementing the glowing golden leaves of prolific self-seeding feverfew (*Tanacetum parthenium* 'Aureum'), which appear early in spring. Taller shrubs include sweet mock orange, *Philadelphus coronarius* 'Aureus', with scented white flowers in midsummer; and the evergreen honeysuckle, *Lonicera japonica* 'Aureoreticulata', with golden-green speckled leaves, is clipped into dome-like features along the path edge. The yellow-flowered Welsh poppy, *Meconopsis cambrica* (another seeder), golden-leaved creeping jenny (*Lysimachia nummularia* 'Aurea') and the gold-variegated form of *Lamium maculatum* prolong the yellow and gold motif. Yellow-flushed *Lilium* Golden Splendor and martagon lilies spearing between glaucous-leaved hostas complete the scheme.

This may all sound a bit much, but cut off from other areas of the garden this golden 'picture' is seen in isolation and could be a prototype for any gold garden. In a plan for a larger space with more sun (implemented at Pyrford Court in Surrey) Miss Jekyll recommended additional plants in the same theme. She included plants with golden and gold-variegated leaves; among the former were a golden plane tree (*Platanus × acerifolia* 'Suttneri'), elders (both *Sambucus nigra* 'Aurea' and *S. racemosa* 'Plumosa Aurea'), privet (*Ligustrum ovalifolium* 'Aureum'), *Cassinia fulvida* and golden-leaved box. To these we could temptingly add fresh-foliaged *Physocarpus opulifolius* 'Luteus', with leaves which retain their golden tinge through the summer months, and the golden perennial hop (*Humulus lupulus* 'Aureus'). Among variegated golds she used good backbone plants such as hollies, elaeagnus and euonymus.

Elsewhere in her writing Miss Jekyll recommended having a blue garden next to a golden one, to be followed in its turn by a garden with grey leaves, explaining how the juxtaposition of the colours would enhance the effect of each scheme. Gold and yellow complement blues, so when they are placed side by side each of them appears more vivid. Grey makes all associated colours glow more boldly.

However, at Tintinhull I think I would prefer the preparation for the white garden to be a quiet area of more solemn green.

A Golden Scheme 75

A White Garden

White 'Iceberg' roses with white Japanese anemones and Lysimachia ephemerum *perform late beside the spikes of glaucous grass,* Helictotrichon sempervirens. *'Iceberg' has its first flush of flowering in early summer, but flowers again later if carefully deadheaded.*

R INGED BY YEW HEDGES and invisible until the last approach – except in late summer, when a froth of white Japanese anemones crowds the edges of beds to break the vista – the white garden consists of four equal triangular beds and a central pavement framing a circular pool. The planting is quite formal, with repetitive, rather than mirror-image, groups of silver- and grey-leaved plants with white or pale flowers. In this part of the garden none of the beds gets full sun and the yew hedges cast bands of shade. Standard globe-shaped willows – the small silver-leaved *Salix helvetica* – are placed in the corners where the hedges meet. Pruned into shape each winter, they act as architectural features and, after ten years' growth, rise above the horizontal level of the clipped hedges. They will soon need to be replaced. These silvery-leaved willows, along with leptospermums and artemisias, and the variegated ivies (*Hedera helix* 'Glacier') used as edging, separate the dark green of the yews from the flowers, toning down extreme contrasts and considerably reducing the glare of the white effects. We have introduced these silvers gradually in the last ten years.

Over the time we have been tending the beds we have tried to return to a planting scheme more like Mrs Reiss's original intention. As we have frequently been told by visitors that Mrs Reiss had always used pale-tinted flowers and had never envisaged the garden as specifically a 'white' one, we have felt free to experiment. The garden is still basically white, but most of the bulbs, shrubs, roses, perennials and annuals have off-white or creamy flowers rather than the more startling pure white. For example, when we came in 1979 'Iceberg' roses dominated the planting, to make a great show in summer. We have removed some of these and instead planted the more gentle-toned cream rose 'Margaret Merril', with its slight wafting fragrance. Other plants have been chosen to extend the season into the latter part of the summer. However, we may have made a mistake in that, instead of completely reorganizing all the four beds, we have restored and 'improved' them piecemeal, adding plants each year. The garden might look better if, at some appropriate moment, we had made a new plan and redone the planting as a whole scheme.

In this part of the garden the flowering season opens with the ivory flowers of tulip 'Purissima'. There are several groups, along with scattered clumps of white honesty (*Lunaria annua alba*), followed by a white-flowered Brompton stock (*Matthiola incana*), the latter replaced annually from cuttings or seed sown in the open

in June. The seeds from the previous year's biennial honesty germinate by March, so must not be buried in a thick carpet of mulch.

Other early-summer flowers include cream *Primula* 'Lady Greer' in a relatively damp shady corner, and in sun a white variety of grey-leaved *Lychnis coronaria* the latter unreliable as a perennial but encouraged to replace itself by annual seeding *in situ*. In the three more open beds there are massed plantings of white campanulas. The glossy foliage of a creamy water lily, *Nymphaea odorata*, almost fills the pool, and pots of *Senecio smithii* sit on a ledge submerged by water. These moisture-loving plants from Chile and the Falkland Islands, with grey-green puckered leaves, have 30cm/12in stems carrying white yellow-centred daisies.

Important features are two beds set in the paving. In these a white-flowered form of agapanthus (*Agapanthus campanulatus* var. *albidus*), with greenish buds and decorative seedheads, making thick clumps after forty years of being undisturbed, flowers reliably every August. A few Venus' fishing rods (*Dierama pulcherrimum*), also known as wand flowers, have seeded among the agapanthus, where they get adequate drainage and full sun to flower in July. Covering a range from deep pink to blush, their flowers offer a welcome touch of colour among the near-whites. They are also volunteer seeders, but care must be taken not to weed out the tiny tufted grass-like seedlings, happily germinating in cracks in paving during spring.

We found *Lysimachia ephemerum* in the two sunniest beds. With glaucous leaves all summer and delicate white flowers on tall stems in autumn, it is one of the best perennials. In a shady corner we have added one of my other favourite perennials, the invasive creeping *L. clethroides*, with arching white flower spikes. These, with the white anemones (*Anemone* × *hybrida* 'Honorine Jobert') and the delicate *Allium tuberosum*, with chive-like leaves, carry the garden into autumn. White colchicums (*Colchicum speciosum* 'Album') flower in September. In spring we usually add some summer hyacinth bulbs (*Galtonia candicans*), as few seem to survive the winters. I also intend to plant another late-flowering bulb, the charming *Gladiolus callianthus* 'Murieliae' (more familiar as *Acidanthera murieliae*), with sweetly scented flowers and grassy leaves.

For me as for many others, the ideal white garden is the one at Sissinghurst. Here is a garden where the quality and texture of the leaves is as noticeable as the flowers. Moreover, especially when viewed from the tower above, the Sissinghurst white garden clearly demonstrates the importance of design. As well as the geometric box-edged beds arranged around the central rose-covered bower, there are blocks of silver and green foliage plants set out to give quite a formal effect.

At Tintinhull the yew hedges make a fine background, but ideally I would like to edge the beds with box. It is always a good move to hide the unsightly bases of roses and late-summer perennials – in a small area every fading leaf or defect of growth is very visible. I would also grow blocks of flowers rather than naturalistic clumps. I might grow no roses but get my effects from flowers such as arum lilies (*Zantedeschia aethiopica*), summer hyacinths (*Galtonia candicans*) and, in the sunniest corner, a huge mound of spreading

In a corner of the white garden a silvery willow and white 'Iceberg' roses glow against the dark yew hedge. White delphiniums and white Lychnis coronaria *are followed by white Japanese anemones; silver-foliaged plants soften the effect.*

romneya with grey foliage and papery poached-egg flowers. Blocks of *Lotus hirsutus*, blue-leaved rue (*Ruta graveolens* 'Jackman's Blue'), silvery stachys and white lavender (the large *Lavandula angustifolia* 'Alba', which is heavily scented) could alternate with white galega, regale lilies, white dictamnus, a white-flowered form of *Salvia officinalis* (admired at Mottisfont), all of which have attractive leaves and habit even when not flowering. In my garden at Bettiscombe I am planning to include a white area with very few white flowers – in general I want few perennials and hope to get effects with shrubs, bulbs and annuals. On my hottest brick wall a white wisteria for spring will accompany a white Banksian rose; there will be a white *Solanum jasminoides* 'Album' for later in the summer. The last two are slightly tender, but the garden is sheltered and it is only five miles from the English Channel. Grey-leaved olive trees and olearias with white flowers will be undercarpeted with glossy green *Acanthus mollis latifolius* with pale pink flower spikes in summer. As Miss Jekyll wrote in *Colour Schemes for the Flower Garden*, 'It is a curious thing that people will sometimes spoil some garden project for the sake of a word. For instance, a blue garden … may be hungering for a group of white lilies … but it is not allowed to have it because it is called the blue garden and there must be no flowers in it but blue flowers. I can see no sense in this … Surely the business of the blue garden is to be beautiful as well as to be blue. My own idea is that it should be beautiful first, and then just as blue as may be consistent with its best possible beauty.'

Agapanthus campanulatus var. *albidus*

Lunaria annua alba

Rosa 'Margaret Merril'

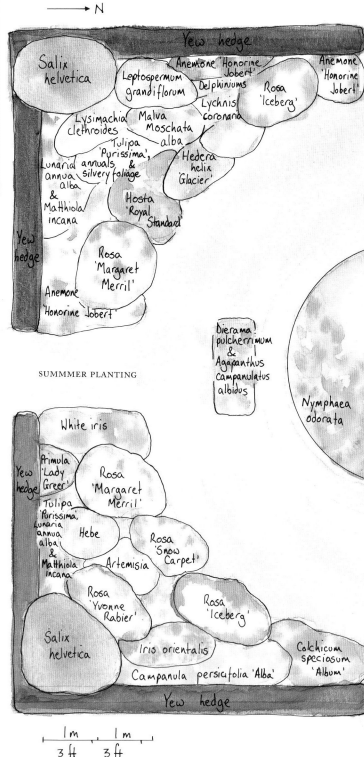

Dierama pulcherrimum

Colchicum speciosum 'Album'

N →

Yew hedge

Salix helvetica

Anemone 'Honorine Jobert'

Leptospermum grandiflorum

Delphiniums

Rosa 'Iceberg'

Anemone 'Honorine Jobert'

Lychnis coronaria

Lysimachia clethroides

Malva moschata alba

Tulipa 'Purissima', annuals & silvery foliage

Hedera helix 'Glacier'

Lunaria annua alba & Matthiola incana

Hosta 'Royal Standard'

Rosa 'Margaret Merril'

Anemone 'Honorine Jobert'

Yew hedge

SUMMMER PLANTING

Dierama pulcherrimum & Agapanthus campanulatus albidus

Nymphaea odorata

White iris

Yew hedge

Primula 'Lady Greer'

Rosa 'Margaret Merril'

Tulipa 'Purissima', Lunaria annua alba & Matthiola incana

Hebe

Rosa 'Snow Carpet'

Artemisia

Rosa 'Yvonne Rabier'

Rosa 'Iceberg'

Salix helvetica

Iris orientalis

Colchicum speciosum 'Album'

Campanula persicifolia 'Alba'

Yew hedge

1 m
3 ft
1 m
3 ft

Self seeders
Dierama pulcherrimum
Lunaria annua alba
Lychnis coronaria
Matthiola incana

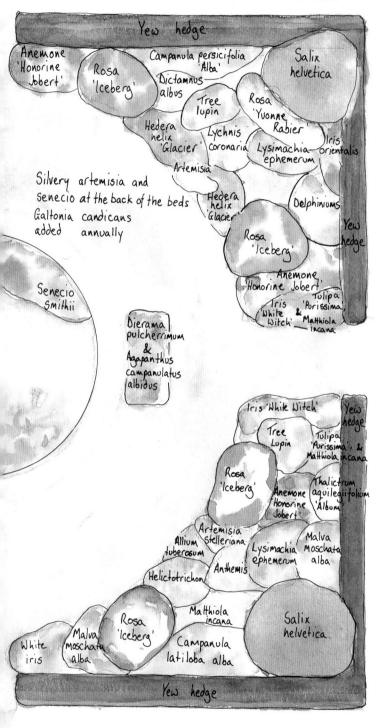

Top bed:

Yew hedge

Anemone 'Honorine Jobert'
Rosa 'Iceberg'
Campanula persicifolia 'Alba'
Dictamnus albus
Salix helvetica
Tree lupin
Rosa 'Yvonne Rabier'
Hedera helix 'Glacier'
Lychnis coronaria
Lysimachia ephemerum
Iris orientalis
Artemisia
Hedera helix 'Glacier'
Delphiniums
Rosa 'Iceberg'
Yew hedge
Anemone 'Honorine Jobert'
Iris 'White Witch'
Tulipa 'Purissima' & Matthiola incana

Silvery artemisia and senecio at the back of the beds
Galtonia candicans added annually

Senecio smithii

Dierama pulcherrimum & Agapanthus campanulatus albidus

Bottom bed:

Iris 'White Witch'
Yew hedge
Tree Lupin
Tulipa 'Purissima' & Matthiola incana
Rosa 'Iceberg'
Anemone 'Honorine Jobert'
Thalictrum aquilegiifolium 'Album'
Artemisia stelleriana
Allium tuberosum
Lysimachia ephemerum
Malva moschata alba
Anthemis
Helictotrichon
Rosa 'Iceberg'
Matthiola incana
Salix helvetica
White iris
Malva moschata alba
Campanula latiloba alba
Yew hedge

Galtonia candicans

Lychnis coronaria

Nymphaea odorata

Matthiola incana

A Foliage Garden

The THIRD compartment in the Fountain Garden is reserved almost entirely for foliage plants. It has little to do with Mrs Reiss but was planted with inspiration by Paul Miles, during his time as a National Trust Gardens' adviser, now fifteen or more years ago. No one seems to know what was there before his time.

After some bad winters many of the Miles plants have died off, but the theme of his planting remains. The area is dominated by the fine pair of giant dogwoods (*Cornus controversa* 'Variegata') with tabulated layered branches, showing off the cream-edged leaves carried on red-tinged stems. The dogwoods have grown to 3.5m/12ft, rising high above the yew hedges. Beneath the trees are glaucous and variegated hostas, rodgersias, biennial Scotch thistles (*Onopordum acanthium*) and Jackman's rue. Three mop-headed hortensia hydrangeas, *Hydrangea macrophylla* 'Générale Vicomtesse de Vibraye', have clear blue flowers carried early in the season. White *Anemone × hybrida* 'Honorine Jobert' and blue-flowered willow gentians (*Gentiana asclepiadea*) perform late.

A large *Phlomis anatolica* occupies one corner by the white seat and *Brachyglottis* 'Sunshine' the other. Behind the seat a self-clinging vine, *Parthenocissus henryana*, its dark leaves netted with strange silvery veins, and turning scarlet in autumn, covers the brick wall. The general effects depend on leaf colours and textures but there are always plenty of flowers.

On one side of the back wall beyond the bay arbour the flowering season is opened in early spring by the hardy *Viburnum × burkwoodii*, with its scented globular heads of pink-tinted buds unfolding to white. On the other side *Clematis rehderiana*, carrying primrose-yellow cowslip-scented bells from September until the frosts, climbs over a frame alongside the wall.

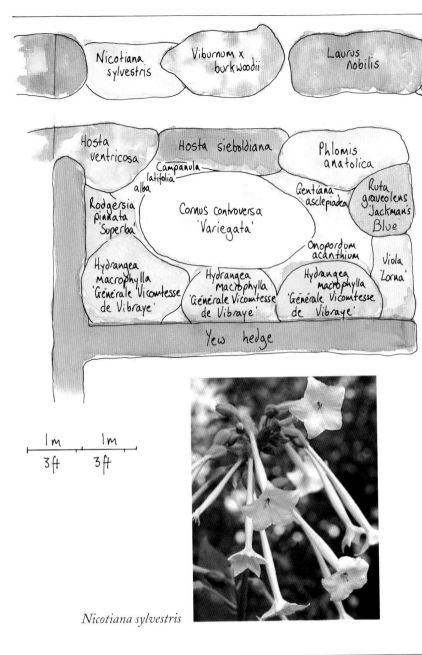

Nicotiana sylvestris

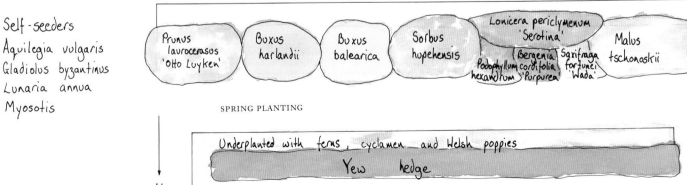

Self-seeders
Aquilegia vulgaris
Gladiolus byzantinus
Lunaria annua
Myosotis

SPRING PLANTING

N

Laurus nobilis

Clematis rehderiana

Clematis 'Miss Bateman'

Akebia quinata

Photinia

Laurus nobilis

Parthenocissus henryana

Hosta ventricosa

Lychnis coronaria alba

Brachyglottis 'Sunshine'

Cornus controversa 'Variegata'

Ajuga reptans

Gentiana asclepiadea 'Alba'

Viola 'Lorna'

Onopordum acanthium

Anemone 'Honorine Jobert'

Yew hedge

In the narrow bed (hardly 45cm/18in wide) under the south wall, there is, besides the crab apples mentioned earlier, a pair of *Sorbus hupehensis*. *Podophyllum hexandrum* and *Saxifraga fortunei* 'Wada' both revel in the shade but need a thick mulch of homemade compost to keep surrounding soil moist. A clump of giant *Astilbe rivularis* proves how effective a large-scale plant can be in a small space. Here it creates a wonderful jungle-like atmosphere, and the invasive roots are contained by paving. Most of these plants have been added since 1979.

Farther along the wall the soil is drier where the roots of the evergreen oaks have spread from the Middle Garden, but the glossy-leaved *Buxus balearica* from the Mediterranean islands and the smaller *B. harlandii*, a dome-shaped bush with bright green leaves, probably originating from China, thrive here in conditions which obviously suit them. They look at home with the oaks.

Lonicera tragophylla

Hydrangea quercifolia

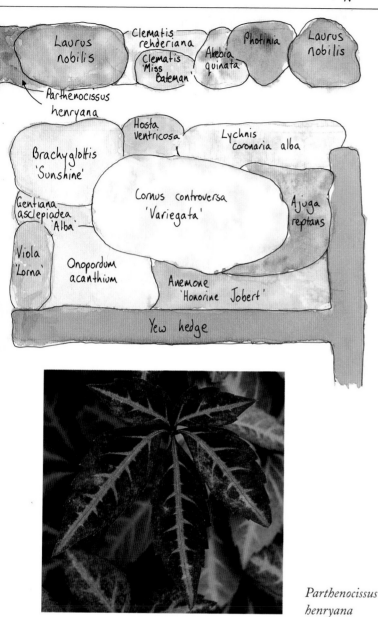

Parthenocissus henryana

Malus tschonoskii

Dryopteris filix-mas

Bergenia

Rosa 'Alchymist'

Clematis montana

Asplenium scolopendrium

Astilbe rivularis

Lonicera tragophylla

Sorbus hupehensis

Old Blush rose

Idesia polycarpa

Pulmonaria longifolia

Laurus nobilis

Hydrangea quercifolia

Underplanted with ferns, cyclamen and Welsh poppies

Yew hedge

Caring for Grey and Silver Plants

GREY AND SILVER foliage plants are a perfect foil to both green and purple-tinged leaves and to all flower colours. While contributing a gentle atmosphere overall, their neutral tones make neighbouring flower or leaf colours seem more vibrant. Arranged in repetitive groups they integrate schemes as firmly as topiary pieces.

At Tintinhull silver and grey plants are used throughout the white beds in the Fountain Garden, and in the Pool Garden plantings of silvery artemisias unite the hot and the pale borders. In the swimming pool border at Royaumont (*opposite above*), where lacy perovskias and artemisias intermingle with clumps of caryopteris, salvias and agapanthus, the silver foliage plants heighten the effects of the flowers.

TAKING CUTTINGS

Silver plants are often slightly tender and may not survive a hard winter, so I take cuttings of semi-mature shoots towards the end of summer.

With *Artemisia arborescens* 'Faith Raven', as with most of the silvery plants, I take heeled shoots (*left*). Some artemisias, such as *A. stelleriana*, often have side shoots which can be pulled from the base of the plant (*top left*). These may well have an embryo root system. All cuttings should be placed at once in an airtight polythene bag (*above left*) and transferred to pots as soon as possible – within a few hours at the most.

Back in the potting shed, I prepare 8cm/3in pots of mixed peat (or a peat alternative) and grit (or perlite). I trim the heeled shoots, or, if they are more than 15cm/6in long, cut across a node where the side shoots join the main stem (*top right*). Then I pinch off the leaves from the lower half of the stem (*above right*), dip the end of the stem in water and press the bare tip into a hormone rooting powder. The cuttings are then placed in the pots, about six to each pot – I use a dibber to make the planting holes (*opposite, below left*). With *A. stelleriana* stems I just pinch off the lower leaves and pop the shoots in the pots (*opposite, below centre*). The soil around the cuttings should be carefully firmed (*opposite, below right*).

I then put the pots in a mist propagator, arranging them on the heated compost surface at the very edge of the mist bench, so that they get just enough spray but not too much. In these conditions cuttings of *A. arborescens* 'Faith Raven', *A.* 'Powis Castle', *A. stelleriana* and most other 'silvers', including the glaucous *Argyranthemum foeniculaceum*, will root in a few weeks. More woody plants such as *Teucrium fruticans* and woolly-leaved willows take longer. Using a mist propagator there is a danger that cuttings may get too moist and rot. It is less risky to root them in an airtight tray or in a pot covered with polythene on a window sill, where condensation will provide all the moisture needed. Cuttings taken from more mature wood can be left to root in a frost-free greenhouse over the winter months. However, at Tintinhull we are always pressed for time and space, and I find that the speed of rooting in the propagator makes up for the extra care needed. As a precaution, we usually keep a stock plant in a pot in the greenhouse during the winter, and take additional cuttings from this in spring, as the days lengthen and new shoots become available.

Artemisia stelleriana is more likely to rot than the taller, lacier artemisias such as *A.* 'Powis Castle' and *A. arborescens* 'Faith Raven' but it is also hardier. Once plants are

cuttings and the compost slip out together, and I gently separate the cuttings – here, of *A.* 'Powis Castle' (*opposite, below left to right*). Holding one in a prepared pot, I add compost around the roots (*left*), fill the pot almost to the top and firm the soil gently around the plant. Then I tease out the remaining plants and pot them on in the same way (*below*). I shall pot on again when the pot seems full of the artemisia's spreading root system, but with a firmer hand, as the potting soil mixture should by now be adhering to the roots in a ball. If it is not, and the ball disintegrates, potting on has been attempted too early.

PLANTING OUT

Before beginning to plant I usually soak the pots and water the ground thoroughly. When planting 'silvers' I do not add fertilizers – these plants like poor situations. I dig a good-sized hole for each plant, tip it

rooted they can be kept in a closed frame over winter, so long as the frame is opened to allow air circulation on fine days.

POTTING ON

After plants have established a root system (you will notice small fibrous roots just emerging from the base), they should be potted on into individual pots. If you use too large a pot there is a risk of overwatering, so choose a pot of an appropriate size and be prepared to pot on again at least once, and sometimes two or three times, before plants can be put out in the open.

I add grit to a proprietary potting compost and put some of the mixture in the bottom of the required number of pots (*opposite above*). Then I give the base of the old pot a sharp tap, so that the rooted

carefully out of its pot and plant it, firming it in well. *A. stelleriana*, which I am planting here (*above*), is one of the few silver-leaved plants which will tolerate dry shade, so it is ideal for growing near the base of a yew hedge or behind taller plants. I use it mainly in the Fountain Garden, where it goes in the shadier corners, leaving the taller *A. arborescens* and *A. a.* 'Faith Raven' to go where there is more light.

The Distinguished Dogwood Family

Dogwoods, or cornels, from Europe, Asia and America, range in size from trees (the Pacific dogwood, *Cornus nuttallii*, and the majestic Asiatic giant dogwood, *C. controversa*) to the sub-shrub *C. canadensis* from North American woods. In between there are many shrubby dogwoods. We grow some of these for their startling red, yellow or green polished young stems, spectacular when bare in winter. Other – often stately – shrubs are grown for their habit or their flowering bracts, foliage or fruit.

C. controversa, with tabulated branches, is beautiful in its green form, and the more commonly grown *C.c.* 'Variegata', its leaves marked with creamy yellow turning to white, is even more striking. The handsome pair of *C.c.* 'Variegata' in the Fountain Garden makes a dramatic feature. Both these and the more delicate American *C. alternifolia* 'Argentea' (above the steps at the garden entrance) have a distinctive habit, growing like tiered wedding cakes. They are at their most impressive against a dark background.

The dogwoods with coloured stems make interesting additions to almost any garden scheme. *C. alba*, from Siberia and China, has forms with several different bark colours. The Westonbirt dogwood, *C.a.* 'Sibirica', has the most brilliant colour of all the red-stemmed varieties, but 'Elegantissima', with deep red young stems, offers the additional interest of cream-variegated leaves through the summer months, and 'Spaethii', with bright red stems, has leaves margined and marked with gold ('Spaethii' is in the purple and gold border in the Cedar Court). The sober plum-red twigs of the European native

Cornus alternifolia 'Argentea'

Cornus alba 'Elegantissima'

hedgerow dogwood, *C. sanguinea*, being less exotic-looking, are suitable for a natural pond area, as are the deeper, almost violet-plum twigs of *C. stolonifera* (*C. sericea*) from North America. A form of *C. stolonifera*, *C.s.* 'Flaviramea', has greenish-yellow bark. Another American, *C. racemosa*, has white fruits in autumn as well as rose-coloured stems in winter. Most of these dogwoods grown for the colour of their young stems should be cut right back almost to ground level at least every other spring. If you prune *C. racemosa* more selectively, leaving a

Cornus kousa var. *chinensis*

Cornus kousa var. *chinensis*

proportion of the older wood, you will get the fruits too.

Other dogwoods have decorative flowers or coloured bracts. The European Cornelian cherry, *C. mas*, is a woodland plant. It has tiny yellow starry flowers carried before the leaves unfurl in early spring. Fruits follow but are generally hidden by the leaves, which colour well in autumn. In a warm, sheltered garden, the tender evergreen *C. capitata* may eventually become a small tree; it has creamy-sulphur flower bracts followed by fleshy strawberry-like fruits. A hardier alternative is the superb *C. kousa* or its more lime-tolerant variety *C.k.* var. *chinensis*, both with creamy bracts turning slightly pink and with notable autumn colour. At Tintinhull Mrs Reiss angled the view of the *C.k.* var. *chinensis* in the Cedar Court so that it could be seen from the Courtyard on arrival. It grows fast, and there are several variants, including the semi-evergreen 'Norman Hadden', probably a hybrid between *C. kousa* and *C. capitata*. Sadly, the American dogwood *C. florida* prefers hotter summers and more acid soil than we can provide at Tintinhull and seldom performs to its true potential in Britain, even in the mildest regions. The Pacific dogwood, *C. nuttallii* from the Pacific west coast, a magnificent tree in its native habitat, is even firmer in its preference for acid soil. The little stoloniferous bunchberry, *C. canadensis*, is a woodlander for acid soils, where it will spread into drifts, starred with white flowers, among other typical plants from north-east America, all of which I love but in my neutral to alkaline soil can never grow.

Different Daisies

THE DAISY-FLOWERED Compositae family includes among its members many wonderful garden plants. The daisies grown as annuals are invaluable in beds and containers, loving sun, withstanding drought and having long flowering periods. Some of them will grow to 2.5m/8ft in a season. For a children's garden I designed in America – a temporary affair – our theme came from one of Monet's paintings, with tall dramatic 'avenues' of sunflowers (*Helianthus annuus*) creating secret shady tunnels.

But not all Compositae have wide daisy flowers with distinctive ray florets; some members of the group are grown mainly for their leaves, with little button rayless flowers so clustered in dense heads as to be almost unrecognizable as true daisies. Among these are some of the helichrysums. The drought-tolerant *Helichrysum petiolare* has soft silver leaves on twisting stems which spread out over the edge of containers, while allowing more colourful plants to twine in between. Other shrubby helichrysums with interesting foliage (*H. italicum*, the curry plant, for instance) look marvellous massed in sunny beds or grown in pots. Many of the silver-leaved artemisias can be treated in the same way.

The biennial Scotch thistle, *Onopordum acanthium*, with silvery-grey fiercely armed foliage and stem, is an architectural plant growing as high as 2.5m/8ft in its second season, so it is ideal to mark a gateway or make a focal point. In the Fountain Garden two of them flank a path, framed against a dark wall of yew. Flowering stems break from near the ground in candelabra fashion, and tiny clustered flower buds open to deep purple shaving brushes. I also love another statuesque biennial, the milk thistle, *Silybum marianum*, with green leaves veined in white. The seeds from both these plants will germinate the following spring to flower a year later.

Many of the tender decorative chrysanthemums have been given a new genus, *Argyranthemum*. Perhaps the most beautiful of these is the almost shrubby glaucous thread-leaved *A. foeniculaceum* of gardens, a variant of the marguerite, with sprays of small white daisy flowers all summer (so long as dying flowers are regularly removed). There are now several *Argyranthemum* cultivars and hybrids with more silvery leaves and flowers in various

Silybum marianum

Osteospermum jucundum

Brachyscome iberidifolia

colours. I especially like 'Mary Wootton', with pale pink flowers, and yellow 'Jamaica Primrose', with wide flowers that appear almost luminous. These plants will grow into sizeable shrubs during a summer season and are well able to cope with the robust cut-and-thrust life of a border, jostled by adjacent plants. Cuttings will root readily in the autumn and should be kept in a frost-free greenhouse or cold frame through the winter. It is easy to train them into standards: just tie the main shoot to a cane and remove any side shoots.

The sub-shrubby perennial osteospermums from South Africa need hot sun, good drainage and protection from wind. Given those prerequisites they will survive temperatures down to -5° to -10°C (23° to 14°F) but it is advisable to take cuttings as an insurance. They will make dense mats in a season. Pink-flowered *Osteospermum jucundum* is reasonably hardy at Tintinhull. The more tender *O. ecklonii* has wide white daisies, the ray florets backed in dusky blue, with centres of dark blue. Gazanias, also from South Africa, like similar conditions but are less shrubby in habit.

Blue marguerites from South Africa, species and cultivars of *Felicia*, both *F. amelloides* and its various forms, and the Swan river daisy, *Brachyscome iberidifolia* from Australia, with blue or white flowers, thrive in hot situations and look good in pots. I have always grown felicias from cuttings and brachyscomes from seed.

Zinnias, though now separated from the Compositae into Asteraceae, are still daisies. We usually grow the green-flowered 'Envy', a cultivar of *Zinnia elegans*. Lacking hot sun, we keep it in the greenhouse until it is nearly in flower and grow a group together in a handsome pot by the front door rather than placing it in a mixed planting. I would like to try the unzinnia-looking *Z. angustifolia*, each of its stems surmounted by orange daisies, but do not know if it would enjoy our summers. I have seen it in Texas growing with forms of the ferny-leaved *Tagetes tenuifolia*, known as signet marigold.

Zinnia angustifolia 'Orange Star'

Euphorbias and catmint edge paths in the Kitchen Garden, almost obscuring plantings of more utilitarian vegetables. The view looking east shows the old cedar of Lebanon at the far edge of the Cedar Court. Honeysuckles grown as verticals on metal frames give height – as do shrubs such as hollies and viburnums – while the yew hedge, separating the Kitchen Garden from the Pool Garden, makes a splendid backdrop to the mixed planting.

THE KITCHEN GARDEN

THE KITCHEN GARDEN at Tintinhull remains essentially a working garden, where traditional fruit and vegetables are grown. But, as in the kitchen gardens of the past, seasonal flowers from fruit trees and in borders have a strong influence on its general character.

Twiners grow on wires and tripods to give vertical effects among the low serried rows of more pedestrian vegetables. Sweet peas for cutting and French runner beans with scarlet flowers in summer are in traditional rows, and the more unusual blue hyacinth bean (*Lablab purpureus*, also known as *Dolichos lablab*), with purplish leaves and dark blueish-purple flowers, is exotic on willow frames. The 'cottage' style, with functional paths providing access to beds and with flowers and useful crops almost intermingled, has a charm of its own. It provides a link not only with the grand walled gardens of the past but also with the real cottage gardens of agricultural workers, where vegetables and soft fruit would be grown of necessity, with flowers as decorative additions along path edges.

The Tintinhull Kitchen Garden is attractive enough on its own to provide a model for the main garden area of any modest-sized house. While most of my clients like to have some space for fruit and vegetables, few allow me to mix ornamental plants between or around the rows – although I can usually persuade them to have central pathways lined with catmint, lavender or woody sages, and to use rosemary and mints in an ornamental way. In the west end of a windswept walled garden I designed on Oronsay, off the west coast of Scotland, crops grow in rows beside the greenhouse. At Wormsley in Oxfordshire the scale is quite different, and grand greenhouses and vegetable and soft fruit beds occupy almost a quarter section of the 2-acre walled garden layout. Another vast assemblage of beds contains flowers for cutting. At Herriard Park in Hampshire, where I helped design a new garden, we planned a herb garden, a garden for vegetables and a greenhouse to look as attractive as the flower garden beside the house. In none of these gardens do the kitchen areas intermix with the more flowery beds. However, at Ston Easton, a country house hotel near Bath, rows of flowers (perennials and annuals) for cutting for the house intermingle with herbs and other vegetables for the kitchen. Hotel guests may enjoy a stroll between rows of peas and beans. At Bettiscombe I intend to make my kitchen garden a separate design feature: ultimately I will grow my favourite vegetables – courgettes, lettuce, small French beans and perhaps early potatoes – in raised beds in an enclosed garden concealed by hornbeam hedges.

The old kitchen garden at Tintinhull measures approximately 64 × 27m/210 × 90ft. Of this, during the last fourteen years, we have stolen from cropping plants a 1.5m/5ft border around the edge. And though the centre beds are used primarily for vegetables we also treat them as a nursery for the whole garden, sowing the seed of annuals and biennials in rows among the lettuce, beans and cabbage.

Above: *On the Isle of Oronsay in Scotland an old walled kitchen garden, dating to the fourteenth century and attached to the Priory, has been turned into mixed ornamental, vegetable and fruit gardens. Although frosts are unlikely, fierce salt winds can devastate the plants, so I installed a network of willow hurdles and privet hedges (backed, until they are established, by windproof netting) to give wind-protection.*

Opposite: *Looking east, past the stone vase at the western edge of the garden and through the yew arch into the Pool Garden. In early spring daffodils, tulips, primroses and forget-me-nots bring seasonal colour to the rose border.*

When we first came we used the outer border for single plants on trial: the planting here too had a nursery atmosphere rather than a feeling of permanency. Over the years, however, the worthwhile plants have been retained and divided to make clumps of their own; shrub roses have grown large, and groundcover seeders and spreaders have established themselves as part of the random and cottagey scene. Many of the new plants have a semi-domestic connotation or are useful herbs, which makes them specially suitable for growing adjacent to vegetables. There are shrub roses with apple-like hips, the gilded rosemary – a form of *Rosmarinus officinalis* with striped leaves, grown in the sixteenth century – southernwood, lavenders, lovage, *Salvia officinalis*, angelicas (both the stately *Angelica archangelica* for preserving and the less common *A. gigas*, with

The espalier pears have new shoots pruned back in midsummer. They are pruned more severely in the winter while they are dormant. When young, the main lateral and top shoots are encouraged to make the desired pattern of espalier. In maturity, any excess spurs are removed and lateral shoots are tied down to ensure that they stay horizontal.

Sweet peas need frequent cutting if you want them to flower for a long period; a shoot that is allowed to form seed will not continue to flower. Our sweet peas, grown in rich soil on a traditional framework of bamboos, are constantly being cut for the house.

bronze stems, from Asia). In spring, biennial dyer's woad, *Isatis tinctoria*, with grey-green foliage, produces loose racemes of acid-yellow flowers. The invasive double-flowered bouncing bet (*Saponaria officinalis* 'Rosea Plena'), still used for washing valuable old tapestries and crewel work, flowers in August, its roots contained – just – in a far corner.

This garden, on a lower level than all the other areas, is in a cruciform pattern, with gravel paths dividing the vegetable beds into four separate areas. The central axis path is edged with daffodils and catmint and a stone-paved cross path has on either side pink roses backed by rows of espaliered pear trees. Japanese honeysuckle (*Lonicera japonica* 'Halliana') twines on eight ironwork trellis posts to mark the corners of the rose beds. We doubled up the catmint, *Nepeta* 'Six Hills Giant', to form a continuous line along the centre – previously it was widely spaced – and now it makes a truly impressive show. The avenue of misty mauve flowers leads the eye into the orchard beyond the northern boundary and back towards

At Royaumont in the Ile de France, fruit trees have been trained as espaliers and honeysuckles grown on wooden trellis pillars, a theme I adopted from the Kitchen Garden at Tintinhull. The beds were planned for cutting flowers but annual blue and clary salvias and autumn-flowering sedums have proved too attractive to pick.

Towards the end of the summer the red dahlias lined out in the Kitchen Garden bloom brilliantly beside the catmint, in flower for the second time, and herbs. On the willow frames the blue hyacinth bean (Lablab purpureus, *also known as* Dolichos lablab) *is just coming into flower. Nearby, a sowing of forget-me-nots for spring flowering has germinated.*

the Fountain Garden, extending the feeling of distance. The catmint is so strong and vigorous that, using a sharp spade, we were able to cut off the requisite number of extra groups from the existing planting. Delicate aromatic grey-green leaves make low hummocks attractive for eight months of the year. Lax arching stems carry lavender-coloured flowering shoots 1m/3ft high and wide in early June. These are cut back after the flowers fade – probably at the end of the month or even later, depending on the weather – encouraging new foliage growth, followed by a second but less spectacular flowering in late summer.

The old espaliered pears were replaced in 1982: we grow 'Pitmaston Duchess', 'Doyenné du Comice' and 'Williams' Bon Chrétien'. Mrs Reiss had the pink rose 'Else Poulsen', but we have replaced most of these with 'Mevrouw Nathalie Nypels'. Very similar to 'Else Poulsen', with like habit and shining young bronze leaves, although somewhat paler flowers, 'Mevrouw Nathalie Nypels' flowers even more prolifically, and is much less susceptible to disease. We have kept two 'Else Poulsen' at the central corners to remind us of Mrs Reiss's original preference. Below the roses and spilling out on to the paving we grow the small catmint *Nepeta nervosa*, with catkin-like flowers in pale blue. If the dying flower heads are regularly removed it will flower all summer. Bushes of *Caryopteris* × *clandonensis* 'Heavenly Blue' grow between the roses and by the end of summer scatterings of tall *Verbena bonariensis* spear up between roses and caryopteris to make a mauve haze. At the four outer corners of these borders giant silver-leaved cardoons, *Cynara cardunculus*, give architectural focus, while biennial sweet rocket (*Hesperis matronalis*), blue- and pink-flowered columbines and small violas such as *Viola riviniana* and *V.* 'Bowles' Black' seed freely in any of the gaps.

At the south end of the Kitchen Garden the view into the Fountain Garden is framed by ornamental trees: pyramidal pear trees (*Pyrus calleryana* 'Chanticleer') and *Malus* 'John Downie'. At the east end, steps from the pink rose walk lead up through an archway in the yew hedges into the Pool Garden. The view back from the Pool Garden down the steps is one of the most important in the garden, terminated by a stone vase on the west side.

A bird's-eye view of the garden would reveal quite distinct seasonal colours. In spring yellow narcissi line the central axes, by midsummer a mist of blue catmint and pink shrub roses is dominant. Later, shrubs and perennials, often with pink or white flowers, give interest. Many of the ornamentals, added round the edge since Mrs Reiss's day, are evergreen and keep up winter appearances.

The central vegetable beds with cabbages, Brussels sprouts, leeks and spinach (or Swiss chard) do not always look manicured, but as adjacent areas are cleaned and dug (in any available moment) they convey a satisfactory feeling of use and care.

A clump of Allium tuberosum *flowers in late summer between the bushes of rose 'Mevrouw Nathalie Nypels' and verbena. 'Nathalie Nypels' flowers all season if regularly deadheaded.*

In late summer self-seeded musk mallow (Malva moschata) *flowers between the pink roses 'Mevrouw Nathalie Nypels', while* Verbena bonariensis, *bearing flat mauve flowers on tall strong stems, pushes through. Bushes of blue caryopteris are ranked along the back of the beds where the scented honeysuckle* Lonicera japonica *'Halliana' flowers on metal frames.*

Self-seeders
Alchemilla mollis
Anemone blanda
Aquilegia vulgaris
Brunnera macrophylla
Dicentra formosa
Fritillaria meleagris
Helleborus orientalis
Leucojum aestivum
Polystichum setiferum

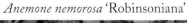
1m 1m
3ft 3ft

Yew hedge

Viburnum carlesii

Rosa gallica officinalis
Scilla siberica
Leucojum aestivum 'Gravetye Giant'

Malus 'John Downie'

Hydrang

Bergenia stracheyi

Senecio doria

Anemone nemorosa 'Robinsoniana'

Lonicera seedling

Paeonia Veitchii

Pulsatilla vulgaris

Daphne Collina

Erythronium

Hemerocallis fulva 'Kwanzo Variegata'

Euphorbia griffithii 'Dixter'

Pulmonaria

Papaver orientale

Teucrium scorodonia

Polystichum setiferum

Pulmonaria

Saxifraga

Anemone nemorosa 'Robinsoniana'

Hemerocallis fulva 'Kwanzo Variegata'

Papaver orientale 'Black and White'

Pulmonaria officinalis 'Sissinghurst White'

Pulmonaria rubra

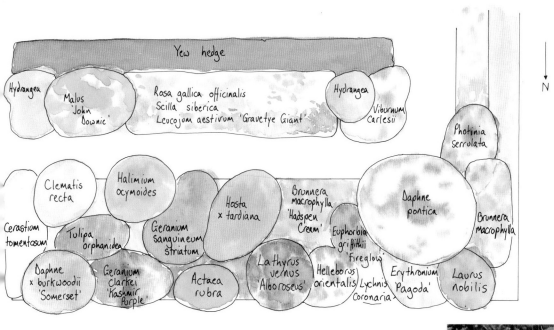

Yew hedge

Hydrangea

Malus 'John Downie'

Rosa gallica officinalis
Scilla siberica
Leucojum aestivum 'Gravetye Giant'

Hydrangea

Viburnum Carlesii

N

Photinia serrolata

Clematis recta

Halimium ocymoides

Hosta × tardiana

Brunnera macrophylla 'Hadspen Cream'

Daphne pontica

Brunnera macrophylla

Cerastium tomentosum

Tulipa orphanidea

Geranium sanguineum striatum

Euphorbia griffithii 'Fireglow'

Daphne × burkwoodii 'Somerset'

Geranium Clarkei 'Kashmir Purple'

Actaea rubra

Lathyrus vernus 'Alboroseus'

Helleborus orientalis

Lychnis coronaria

Erythronium 'Pagoda'

Laurus nobilis

Leucojum aestivum 'Gravetye Giant'

Lathyrus vernus 'Alboroseus'

Cerastium tomentosum

Daphne × *burkwoodii* 'Somerset'

Erythronium 'Pagoda' with *Euphorbia griffithii* 'Fireglow'
and *Daphne pontica*

Lonicera japonica 'Halliana'

Stipa gigantea

Vinca difformis

Euphorbia characias ssp. *wulfenii*
'John Tomlinson'

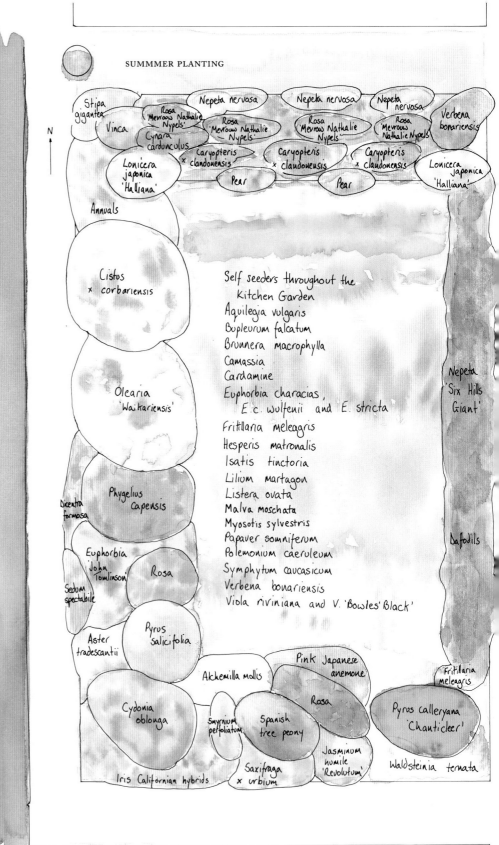

SUMMMER PLANTING

N

Stipa gigantea
Vinca
Rosa 'Mevrouw Nathalie Nypels'
Nepeta nervosa
Nepeta nervosa
Nepeta nervosa
Verbena bonariensis
Cynara cardunculus
Rosa 'Mevrouw Nathalie Nypels'
Rosa 'Mevrouw Nathalie Nypels'
Rosa 'Mevrouw Nathalie Nypels'
Caryopteris × clandonensis
Caryopteris × clandonensis
Caryopteris × clandonensis
Lonicera japonica 'Halliana'
Lonicera japonica 'Halliana'
Pear
Pear

Annuals

Cistus × corbariensis

Olearia 'Waikariensis'

Dicentra formosa

Phygelius capensis

Euphorbia 'John Tomlinson'

Sedum spectabile

Rosa

Aster tradescantii

Pyrus salicifolia

Cydonia oblonga

Smyrnium perfoliatum

Alchemilla mollis

Pink Japanese anemone

Rosa

Spanish tree peony

Jasminum humile 'Revolutum'

Saxifraga × urbium

Iris Californian hybrids

Pyrus calleryana 'Chanticleer'

Waldsteinia ternata

Fritillaria meleagris

Nepeta 'Six Hills Giant'

Daffodils

Self seeders throughout the
Kitchen Garden
Aquilegia vulgaris
Bupleurum falcatum
Brunnera macrophylla
Camassia
Cardamine
Euphorbia characias,
E.c. wulfenii and E. stricta
Fritillaria meleagris
Hesperis matronalis
Isatis tinctoria
Lilium martagon
Listera ovata
Malva moschata
Myosotis sylvestris
Papaver somniferum
Polemonium caeruleum
Symphytum caucasicum
Verbena bonariensis
Viola riviniana and V. 'Bowles' Black'

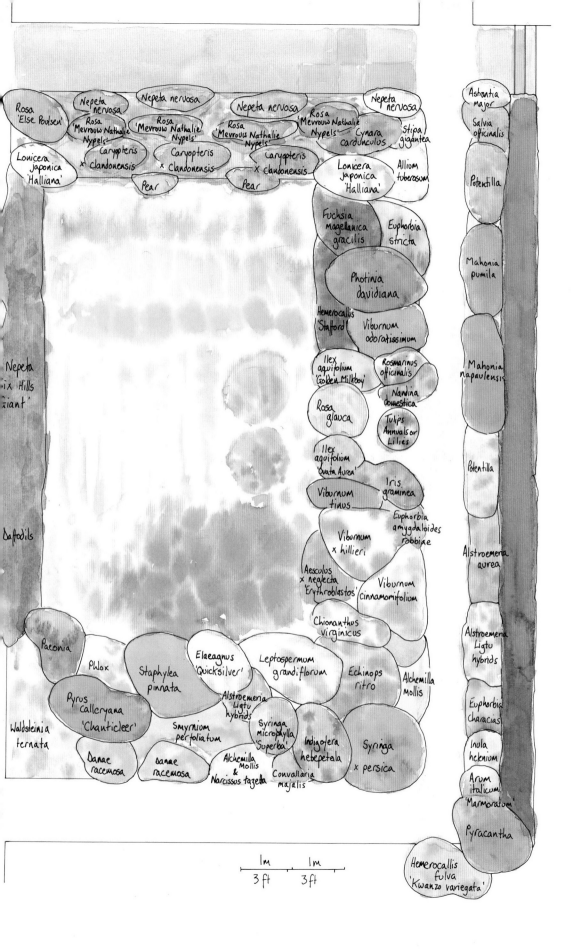

Rosa 'Else Poulsen'

Nepeta nervosa

Nepeta nervosa

Nepeta nervosa

Nepeta nervosa

Rosa 'Mevrouw Nathalie Nypels'

Rosa 'Mevrouw Nathalie Nypels'

Rosa 'Mevrouw Nathalie Nypels'

Rosa 'Mevrouw Nathalie Nypels'

Cynara cardunculus

Stipa gigantea

Caryopteris × clandonensis

Caryopteris × clandonensis

Caryopteris × clandonensis

Lonicera japonica 'Halliana'

Allium tuberosum

Lonicera japonica 'Halliana'

Pear

Pear

Fuchsia magellanica gracilis

Euphorbia stricta

Photinia davidiana

Hemerocallis 'Stafford'

Viburnum odoratissimum

Ilex aquifolium 'Golden Milkboy'

Rosmarinus officinalis

Nandina domestica

Rosa glauca

Tulips Annuals or Lilies

Ilex aquifolium 'Ovata Aurea'

Iris graminea

Viburnum tinus

Euphorbia amygdaloides robbiae

Viburnum × hillieri

Aesculus × neglecta 'Erythroblastos'

Viburnum cinnamomifolium

Chionanthus virginicus

Nepeta 'Six Hills Giant'

Daffodils

Paeonia

Phlox

Staphylea pinnata

Elaeagnus 'Quicksilver'

Leptospermum grandiflorum

Echinops ritro

Alchemilla Mollis

Pyrus calleryana 'Chanticleer'

Alstroemeria Ligtu hybrids

Smyrnium perfoliatum

Syringa microphylla 'Superba'

Indigofera hebepetala

Syringa × persica

Waldsteinia ternata

Danae racemosa

Danae racemosa

Alchemilla Mollis & Narcissus tazetta

Convallaria majalis

Astrantia major

Salvia officinalis

Potentilla

Mahonia pumila

Mahonia napaulensis

Potentilla

Alstroemeria aurea

Alstroemeria Ligtu hybrids

Euphorbia characias

Inula helenium

Arum italicum 'Marmoratum'

Pyracantha

Hemerocallis fulva 'Kwanzo variegata'

1m
3 ft

1m
3 ft

Rosa 'Else Poulsen'

Caryopteris × clandonensis

Aesculus × neglecta 'Erythroblastos'

Smyrnium perfoliatum

Crinum × powellii

Symphytum caucasicum

Gaura lindheimeri

Aster ericoides

Angelica archangelica

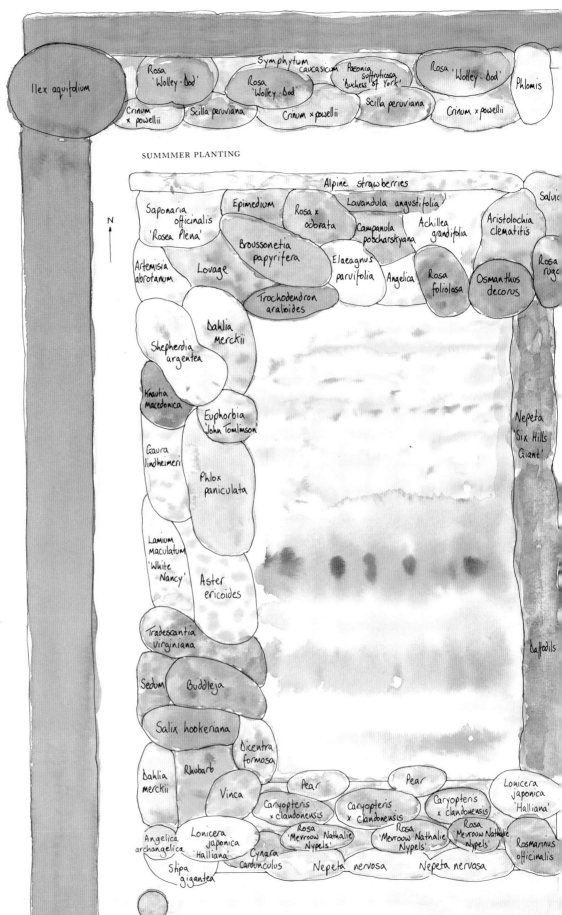

Ilex aquifolium

Rosa 'Wolley-Dod'

Symphytum caucasicum

Rosa 'Wolley-Dod'

Paeonia suffruticosa 'Duchess of York'

Rosa 'Wolley-Dod'

Phlomis

Crinum × powellii

Scilla peruviana

Crinum × powellii

Scilla peruviana

Crinum × powellii

SUMMER PLANTING

N

Alpine strawberries

Saponaria officinalis 'Rosea Plena'

Epimedium

Rosa × odorata

Lavandula angustifolia

Campanula poscharskyana

Achillea grandifolia

Aristolochia clematitis

Salvia

Artemisia abrotanum

Lovage

Broussonetia papyrifera

Elaeagnus parvifolia

Angelica

Rosa foliolosa

Osmanthus decorus

Rosa ruga

Trochodendron araloides

Shepherdia argentea

Dahlia Merckii

Knautia macedonica

Euphorbia 'John Tomlinson'

Gaura lindheimeri

Phlox paniculata

Nepeta 'Six Hills Giant'

Lamium maculatum 'White Nancy'

Aster ericoides

Tradescantia virginiana

Sedum

Buddleja

Salix hookeriana

Dicentra formosa

Dahlia merckii

Rhubarb

Vinca

Pear

Pear

Lonicera japonica 'Halliana'

Caryopteris × clandonensis

Caryopteris × clandonensis

Caryopteris × clandonensis

Angelica archangelica

Lonicera japonica 'Halliana'

Rosa 'Mevrouw Nathalie Nypels'

Rosa 'Mevrouw Nathalie Nypels'

Rosa 'Mevrouw Nathalie Nypels'

Rosmarinus officinalis

Stipa gigantea

Cynara Cardunculus

Nepeta nervosa

Nepeta nervosa

daffodils

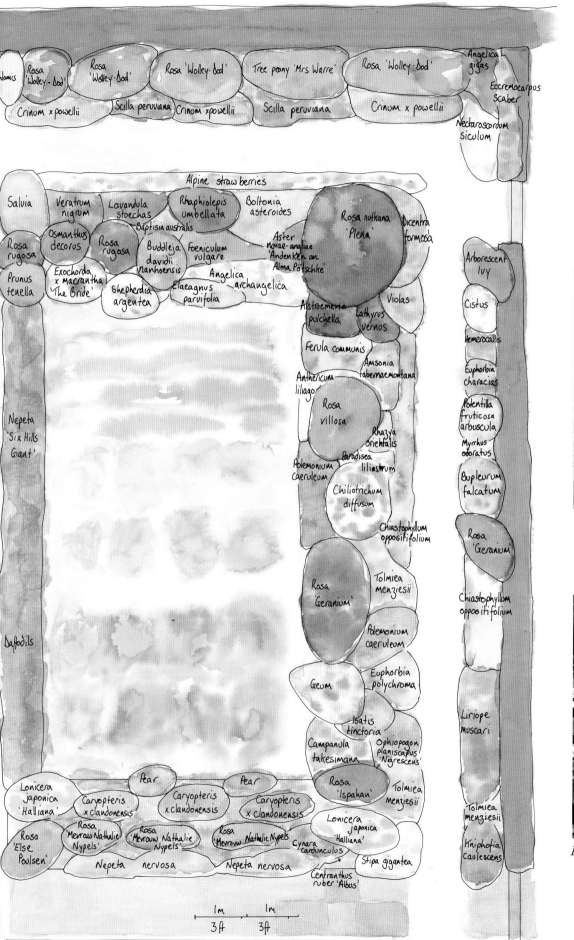

Phlomis
Rosa 'Wolley-Dod'
Rosa 'Wolley-Dod'
Rosa 'Wolley-Dod'
Tree peony 'Mrs Warre'
Rosa 'Wolley-Dod'
Angelica gigas
Eccremocarpus scaber
Crinum × powellii
Scilla peruviana
Crinum × powellii
Scilla peruviana
Crinum × powellii
Nectaroscordum siculum

Alpine strawberries

Salvia
Veratrum nigrum
Lavandula stoechas
Rhaphiolepis umbellata
Boltonia asteroides
Rosa nutkana 'Plena'
Dicentra formosa
Osmanthus decorus
Baptisia australis
Rosa rugosa
Rosa rugosa
Buddleja davidii nanhoensis
Foeniculum vulgare
Aster novae-angliae 'Andenken an Alma Pötschke'
Prunus tenella
Exochorda × macrantha 'The Bride'
Shepherdia argentea
Elaeagnus parvifolia
Angelica archangelica
Alstroemeria pulchella
Lathyrus vernus
Violas
Ferula communis
Amsonia tabernaemontana
Anthericum liliago
Rosa villosa
Rhazya orientalis
Paradisea liliastrum
Polemonium caeruleum
Chiliotrichum diffusum
Chiastophyllum oppositifolium
Nepeta 'Six Hills Giant'
Rosa 'Geranium'
Tolmiea menziesii
Polemonium caeruleum
Euphorbia polychroma
Geum
Daffodils
Isatis tinctoria
Campanula takesimana
Ophiopogon planiscapus 'Nigrescens'
Pear
Pear
Rosa 'Ispahan'
Tolmiea menziesii
Lonicera japonica 'Halliana'
Caryopteris × clandonensis
Caryopteris × clandonensis
Caryopteris × clandonensis
Lonicera japonica 'Halliana'
Rosa 'Else Poulsen'
Rosa 'Mevrouw Nathalie Nypels'
Rosa 'Mevrouw Nathalie Nypels'
Rosa 'Mevrouw Nathalie Nypels'
Cynara cardunculus
Stipa gigantea
Nepeta nervosa
Nepeta nervosa
Centranthus ruber 'Albus'

Arborescent Ivy
Cistus
Hemerocallis
Euphorbia characias
Potentilla fruticosa arbuscula
Myrrhus odoratus
Bupleurum falcatum
Rosa 'Geranium'
Chiastophyllum oppositifolium
Liriope muscari
Tolmiea menziesii
Kniphofia caulescens

1m   1m
3ft   3ft

Paeonia suffruticosa 'Mrs Warre'

Crinum × powellii 'Album'

Scilla peruviana

Rhaphiolepis umbellata

Ophiopogon planiscapus 'Nigrescens'

The Gallica Rose Beds and the Dry Ridge

On the south side of the Kitchen Garden, beneath the yew hedge that separates it from the Fountain Garden, two rectangular beds are planted with a carpet of *Rosa gallica* var. *officinalis*, the apothecary's rose. This is another of Mrs Reiss's inspired ideas, well worth copying in other gardens.

The apothecary's rose, also known as the red rose of Lancaster, has richly scented semi-double rosy-crimson flowers, with prominent yellow anthers. A sport of the deep pink *Rosa gallica*, a rose grown in Europe from the earliest recorded times, it has been known in cultivation since the fourteenth century. Produced after the main flush of midsummer roses, the flowers last about three weeks provided they are not damaged by rain. After flowering is over things are less satisfactory. The flower heads should be removed, for aesthetic reasons; if this task is neglected, the rose looks a mess.

There is a standard *Viburnum carlesii* positioned at the far end of each bed. Blue scillas make a carpet beneath the roses in early spring and by April *Leucojum aestivum*, the summer snowflake, is flowering as freely as it would in a damp meadow, each 60cm/2ft stem holding its flower head above the developing roses. Its white bell-shaped flowers resemble snowdrops but have out-turned green tips and hang in a loose cluster. The form we grow is the best, *L.a.* 'Gravetye Giant', which had its origin in William Robinson's garden at Gravetye Manor in Sussex. It seeds itself in neighbouring beds.

An old lonicera hedge once grew on the other side of the Gallica rose beds. We removed it, to leave a ridge supported by a low wall. This is the only raised bed in the garden and, well drained and partly shaded, provides ideal conditions for small plants we treasure.

This was always considered a temporary scheme, so it had no planting plan and suitable plants were added on impulse; at first around the base of the hedge and later to fill the available space. At the eastern end, where there is some shade and moisture, a clump of the variegated form of the old daylily *Hemerocallis fulva* 'Kwanzo Variegata' makes a focal point at the end of the long eastern path. It is a coarse plant but in early spring its leaves are valuable. *Bergenia stracheyi* from the Himalaya, a miniature elephant's ears with rounded leaves, makes neat rosettes on the edge of the bed. A temperamental plant, it has white flowers, decorated by green calyces in spring. Near it is a clump of *Euphorbia griffithii* 'Dixter'. Similar to the popular *E.g.* 'Fireglow', with vivid brick-red bracts and colourful leaves, which thrives at the far end of the ridge, it is more muted, with a reddish tinge to the foliage. Next comes a

Above: The apothecary's rose looks wonderful when in flower, massed in the bed in front of the yew hedge. Using one plant in quantity is an effective way of making a section of the garden appear much larger than it really is. On the dry ridge opposite, Halimium ocymoides *flowers beside* Geranium sanguineum var. striatum.

Opposite: On the ridge at the south end of the Kitchen Garden planting is very tight. In spring hellebores seed among the brunnera under the skirts of a large Daphne pontica, *and* Euphorbia griffithii *'Fireglow' spreads among erythroniums. Summer snowflakes flower in the back bed.*

rough-leaved perennial, *Senecio doria*, with bright yellow daisies in summer – less desirable but easier to grow than purple-flowered *S. pulcher*, which we lost. *Paeonia veitchii* from China is small and slow to establish. It is seldom more than 30cm/12in high, with suckering stems bearing finely cut leaves and pink flowers with cream anthers in late spring. If there were space I would like to have many more species peonies. The ferny leaves of the native pasque flower, *Pulsatilla vulgaris*, found on chalk downs, emerge early to protect the soft silky buds and purple flowers with golden stamens. Later the copper-brown seedheads are as attractive. There are erythroniums and white- and pink-flowered forms of *Pulmonaria saccharata*. Snow-in-summer (*Cerastium tomentosum*) carpets a corner of the steps. *Tulipa orphanidea* Whittallii Group was a gift; it is quite modest, with slender flowers of dull red with a green mark on the outside of the segments. Nearby is an exuberant purple-flowered *Geranium clarkei* 'Kashmir Purple', which flowers prolifically in late spring, and there are small-leaved hostas (such as

the glaucous *Hosta × tardiana*) and a variegated form of blue-flowered brunnera (*Brunnera macrophylla* 'Hadspen Cream'). By April the delicate cut foliage of baneberry, *Actaea rubra*, from north-east America, is spearing through the soil. In July, after bearing fluffy white flowers, the actaea has clusters of poisonous pea-sized green berries which quickly turn a glowing red. (A white-berried form is even more desirable.) There is *Daphne × burkwoodii* 'Somerset', with pinkish highly scented flowers in sun, and in shade a vast bush of the evergreen yellow-flowered *Daphne pontica*, its flowers fragrant in the evening. Other plants and seedlings include leucojums, alchemillas, and snakeshead fritillaries (*Fritillaria meleagris*) volunteered from nearby beds. Drought-loving deciduous ferns grow in the shadiest parts of the low walls. The effects are random and cottagey, almost a relief from the more ordered colour schemes and plant themes found in most of the garden. However, this sort of 'natural' planting needs constant care, or fast-growing thugs will overwhelm less vigorous plants.

THE SOUTH BORDERS

AT THE SOUTH END of the garden, under one of the shapely pears, clumps of my favourite Alexandrian laurel, *Danaë racemosa*, with waving fronds of glossy leaves and dark red berries, are beginning to bush out, 1m/3ft high and wide, above lower groundcover. This shade-lover from the Mediterranean region, so often seen in Italian gardens, thrives in hot dry summers. We introduced *Smyrnium perfoliatum*, with acid-yellow bracts, to this part of the garden and it has begun to spread in the light shade under the pears, on one side next to spreading alstroemeria – the Ligtu hybrid pink form – in a patch of sunlight, and on the other next to clumps of multicoloured *Iris* Californian hybrids planted under a quince (*Cydonia oblonga*). The leaves of smyrniums in the first two seasons much resemble ground elder. It does not flower until three years after being sown. Now, after five years, it is flowering annually, and it threatens to overwhelm the lower *Waldsteinia ternata*, which is meant to make a neat square on the two 'pear' corners. Other volunteers have already spoiled the intended symmetry. Seedling martagon lilies, snakeshead fritillaries, wild cardamine or cuckoo spit (a favourite but easily weeded out), tway-blades (*Listera ovata*) and common aquilegias all find the waldsteinia area a perfect breeding ground. I wonder if Phyllis Reiss allowed these intruders? She probably did, and welcomed them. Any plant lists and plans are apt to become sacrosanct once committed to paper and seldom represent the original designer's maturing wishes.

At the edge of these beds, to add height and mark the division between ornamentals and kitchen garden proper, we have added the relatively new (to commerce) *Elaeagnus* 'Quicksilver' (once thought to be a variety of the Russian olive, *E. angustifolia*, but with the suckering habit of the lower-growing *E. commutata*). With its silvery leaves and wonderfully scented yellow flowers, it is spectacular in late spring. It is a better flowerer than *E. angustifolia* but it has a fault, for by late summer it is dropping its leaves and looks as if it is dying. For this reason I hesitate to place it in the gardens of clients and remain faithful to the true Russian olive. Nearby, the upright *Staphylea pinnata* bears drooping white panicles in late spring, followed by baggy green capsules through the summer. This shrub, from south Europe and western Asia, has been grown in Britain since the sixteenth century. On the other side of the path, a tree peony, from seed brought from Spain, has grown tall. Its pink flowers present a foil to the silver elaeagnus leaves. All of this is underplanted with *Alchemilla mollis* and Japanese anemones.

Rose 'Geranium' has scarlet flowers in early summer. These are followed by orange flagon-shaped pendulous fruits which remain decorative for many months. Growing tall and wide at the top, this rose does not make dense shade, so many small plants can be grown next to it. They help to disguise the ugly woody base which develops over a period of years.

THE EASTERN PATHWAY

The old copper container, in light shade, is perfect for summer felicias and Salvia cacaliifolia, *both of which flower for many months. At Bettiscombe I am going to grow the spreading blue grass,* Elymus arenarius, *in the same pot, but in full sun.*

THE EASTERN pathway, running beside a narrow bed under the yew hedge which separates the kitchen area from the Pool Garden, has acquired a character of its own, more or less separating it from the rest of the kitchen area. Evergreen and deciduous shrubs and low perennials flop over each side of the path.

This was the first area in which we planted more experimentally. An alcove with a copper pot, in which are planted tulips followed by summer-flowering annuals (or, more recently, lilies), is framed by two large hollies, *Ilex aquifolium* 'Golden Milkboy' and *I.a.* 'Ovata Aurea', grown to make architectural pyramids, both with startling golden patterns or splashings on their leaves. In the former the gold is in the centre of the leaf, while the latter has green leaves margined with yellow. Taller evergreen shrubs screen this path from the vegetables. *Photinia davidiana* (formerly *Stransvaesia davidiana*) is trained as a standard; *Viburnum* × *hillieri*, tender glossy-leaved *V. odoratissimum* and the sacred Chinese bamboo, *Nandina domestica*, are all mature specimens. The deciduous Persian lilac, *Syringa* × *persica*, has scented mauve flowers in late spring, and the fringe tree, *Chionanthus virginicus*, bears drooping white panicles in early summer. The shrubs along this side of the 'secret' pathway, and the yew hedge on the other, are underplanted with spreading plants. *Arum italicum* 'Marmoratum', with marbled cream and green leaves in winter, shrub-like, glaucous-leaved *Euphorbia characias* and the soft-stemmed *E. amygdaloides* var. *robbiae* are evergreen, as are grassy-leaved *Liriope muscari* and *Chiastophyllum oppositifolium* – a small creeping plant with yellow flower tassels in summer, ideal for edging in half-shade. Also under the shrubs (although it would probably prefer a more open situation), *Iris graminea*, the grassy-leaved plum tart, flowers early. Its apple-scented flowers, nestling in the long leaves, have purple styles and violet falls. On the sunny side, under the yew hedge, the spreading *Alstroemeria aurea* competes with neighbouring Ligtu hybrids in shades of pink.

A pair of grasses, *Stipa gigantea*, with purplish-golden flower heads, arch almost to meet on either side of the entrance to the rose/pear walk, at the bottom of the steps from the Pool Garden. With wands reaching to 2m/7ft, this is my favourite perennial grass, best viewed against a western sky in the evening. Beyond the more open end of the eastern pathway, shrub roses are a feature. One of the most beautiful of the old roses, Damask rose 'Ispahan', with fragrant light pink semi-double flowers, grows on the inner side of the path, as does *Rosa* 'Geranium', with scarlet waxy flowers.

Growing nearby is *R. villosa* (*R. pomifera*), with grey leaves, wide single pink flowers and the largest apple-like hips. The tall large *R. nutkana* 'Plena', better known as *R. californica* 'Plena', with graceful arching branches, grows on a corner; it has grey-green leaves and double pink flowers. Between these large roses grow St Bernard's lilies, *Anthericum liliago* and St Bruno's lilies, *Paradisea liliastrum*. These are very similar, both flowering in early summer with white tubular flowers on spikes, but St Bernard's lilies are taller and more substantial. Both *Rhazya orientalis* from Asia and the closely related North American *Amsonia tabernaemontana*, also in this border, have small starry flowers in misty blue, and untidy grassy leaves. The giant fennel, *Ferula communis*, from the shores of the Mediterranean, has a tracery of delicately divided leaves in spring, from which, occasionally, 2m/7ft stems bear great umbelliferous yellow cow-parsley heads in summer. Tap-rooted, it must be grown from seed and transplanted to its permanent site when young.

The North Borders

At the northern boundary of the Kitchen Garden, in front of the holly hedge, tall bushes of grey-leaved *Rosa* 'Wolley-Dod' (*R. villosa* 'Duplex') have pink flowers in profusion followed by large apple-like fruits. Now 3m/10ft tall, they tower above a line of pink- and white-flowered forms of *Crinum × powellii*. The crinums, beautiful in flower in late summer, are difficult to manage. The leaves come through the ground early and their tips are always scorched by frost, with blemishes remaining all through the season. I have tried throwing over light coverings of some protective material when late frosts are threatened but still have not solved this problem. Grey-leaved comfrey, *Symphytum caucasicum*, contributes pale blue flowers on tall stems which rise behind the crinums in early summer. It is an excellent plant for sun or half-shade, easily grown from seed and distributing itself naturally if allowed to do so.

Lavenders, shrubby sages and alpine strawberries thrive and spread under the light shade of *Elaeagnus parvifolia* and the male form of the rare Chinese paper mulberry, *Broussonetia papyrifera*, which bears long catkins in spring. (In China and Japan the exfoliating bark of large plants was used for making paper and the bark fibre for making cloth.)

Nearby is *R. foliolosa*, a pink North American rose that grows only 1m/3ft high and wide; with no thorns and suckering freely it is suitable, if grown on its own roots, for hedging or massing and – like *R. nitida* and the swamp rose, *R. palustris*, neither grown at Tintinhull – it is a good choice for moist areas. Also in sun at this end of the garden, *Exochorda × macrantha* 'The Bride' flowers early with the daffodils, opening the shrub season with its double white flowers. In the same area false indigo, *Baptisia australis*, with blue pea flowers and grey leaves, flowers in midsummer, black seed pods hanging on until well in the autumn. Close by is one of the last flowers to bloom, daisy-flowered *Boltonia asteroides*, a first cousin to the Michaelmas daisy tribe. It has silvery leaves and yellow-centred white flowers. It grows near the cerise-scarlet *Aster novae-angliae* 'Andenken an Alma Pötschke', the brightest of all Michaelmas daisies.

THE WEST BEDS

O N THE WESTERN fringe of the garden two large *Euphorbia characias* ssp. *wulfenii* 'John Tomlinson' make a magnificent splash, their 30cm/12in flower heads a strong acid-yellow. In my opinion this is a better form than Margery Fish's euphorbia 'Lambrook Gold', its bracts more pointed and its habit more graceful. These giant euphorbias have a short life span and cuttings are taken every spring. Cistus, olearias, late-flowering asters and annuals flourish along this western boundary. We often store summer-flowering perennials here in rows during the winter months; each year a few are kept back as emergency stopgaps for the main borders. A spreading clump of scarlet Cape figwort, *Phygelius capensis*, first came here in this way, and has been allowed to stay.

Below: Angelica archangelica *and silvery cardoons make a handsome setting for the stone vase at the end of the rose walk. Edible plants, with superbly decorative foliage, they link the ornamental appearance of the Kitchen Garden with its more mundane aspect.*

Above: *Orderly rows of potatoes and carrots are edged on one side by catmint and on the other by mixed planting that includes white-flowered* Cistus × corbariensis *and forget-me-nots. The dark-leaved plant is sweet william,* Dianthus barbatus Nigrescens Group, *the foliage of which turns purple after a cold winter. It has been lined out for use in the hot borders in the Pool Garden.*

Left: *The view into the old cider orchard on the north side of the garden is framed by rose 'Wolley-Dod', crinums, Rugosa roses and phlomis species. This vista is the only glimpse of the outside world from the Tintinhull garden.*

Sowing Seed in Open Ground

Forget-me-nots for early spring are planted throughout the garden. They are allowed to seed, germinate and flower in the following season wherever they choose to establish themselves. But the intensity of blue decreases each season, so every few years, in June, we sow a batch of a named myosotis from one of the reliable seed catalogues.

So long as the ground is well prepared, sowing the seed of annuals or biennials is very easy. Our problem is always finding a suitable space for a row in the already packed Kitchen Garden. Stretch a string between two pegs, make a shallow trench with the back of a rake and carefully scatter the fine seed along the row (*above, right and far right*). Rake a little soil over the top but do not firm it in (*right*). Then water the soil, using a watering can with a fine rose

(*below right*). The row should be labelled with the name of the plant and the date of planting – I usually put the label in before I even begin the sowing, as it is so easy to forget to do it afterwards.

By September the young plants have usually made quite a lot of growth (*below left*), and they should be moved to the situations in which they will flower the following spring, so that roots get well established before cold weather sets in. This moving always presents us with another difficulty, as the current year's annuals are still in fine condition and it is difficult to make space without discarding plants which are contributing to the summer display. One solution is to pot up plants individually and keep them in cold frames for the winter, ready to plant out in early spring. In fact it is always advisable to keep some potted plants in reserve in case the winter is severe.

Gardening is never a matter of a cut-and-dried list of tasks – when you are doing one thing you will always see something else that needs attention. When I was watering my forget-me-nots I noticed that the blue hyacinth bean, *Lablab purpureus* (*Dolichos lablab*), was looking a bit dry, so I took the rose off the watering can and gave it a good soaking.

Taking Rose Cuttings

W HILE NURSERYMEN usually feel constrained to graft roses on to a chosen stock rose, in your own garden, free from the necessity to guarantee uniformity of strength and vigour, you can increase your rose supply by rooting cuttings. Not all cultivated roses are sufficiently vigorous to do well on their own roots – highly bred Hybrid Teas, for example, really need to be grafted – but I would certainly recommend taking cuttings of species and other strong-growing roses. Apart from the intrinsic satisfaction, there is also a practical advantage: most roses grown on their own roots will not produce suckers, which can easily develop when a plant is grafted on to a stock rose; and removing suckers is one of the most tedious of garden tasks.

All twenty-four plants of the Polyantha rose 'Mevrouw Nathalie Nypels' in the double border of the Kitchen Garden are from two original plants obtained in 1980. I take cuttings of semi-mature wood around the middle of the summer (*above right*). Using sharp secateurs I cut off non-flowering shoots 20–25cm/8–10in long, making sure they have a heel of the old wood attached (*above, far right*), and pop them quickly into a plastic bag to prevent them drying out. In the potting shed I snip off some of the upper leaves (*right*), remove the lower leaves and trim off the heel with a razor blade or a very sharp knife. Alternatively, I cut up pieces of longer stems, making the base cut just below one node (where the leaves join the stem) and the upper cut just above another. I then plunge the whole shoot in a fungicide to prevent disease, and dip the rooting end into a hormone rooting powder to stimulate root growth.

About six semi-mature cuttings should fit around the edge of an 8cm/3in pot filled with a mixture of peat (or peat alternative), loam and vermiculite (*below right*). It is possible to root in pure vermiculite, but I use loam as it provides some nutrition for the young cuttings if I am too busy to pot on as soon as they have rooted. I keep the cuttings in a mist propagator with underheating, positioning them where they will be kept moist, but not drowned. New young shoots on the cuttings indicate that a viable root system has been established. In the moist warmth of the propagator cuttings taken at midsummer usually develop roots by early autumn, and at that point I pot them up individually. They are then transferred to a cold frame for the winter. They can be planted out the following spring, to perform in their first year.

Alternatively, hardwood cuttings can be taken in autumn. They are treated in the same way as semi-mature cuttings, except that they are planted out about 20cm/8in apart in an open trench with some coarse sand at the bottom to encourage rooting. Or they may be kept covered in a closed airtight frame. They will be rooted by the spring, but should be left undisturbed until the following autumn when they can be potted up.

Using Shrub Roses

Shrub roses are infinitely useful in the garden. Both the 'old' roses – including species and varieties, most often garden crosses already centuries old – and the more modern hybrids have distinctive characteristics which make them striking as garden features. At the same time, with their lax but graceful habit, they fit effectively into mixed planting schemes, happily associating with other shrubs – such as viburnums, deutzias and philadelphus – and with soft-stemmed herbaceous plants.

Shrub roses are year-round plants, their shapes and stems, and sometimes beautiful fruits, gracing the garden even in winter. In spring the arching branches protect spring-flowering bulbs. Summer foliage effects are very variable: leaves can be mat (most of the Gallicas) or glossy green, glaucous purple-flushed grey (*R. glauca*) or silvery grey (*R. × alba* and *R. villosa* types) to fresh crinkled apple-green (most of the Rugosas); occasionally they are fragrant (*R. eglanteria*). The old species and garden hybrids have a limited flowering period, with a main flush in early or midsummer. Their flowers, often deliciously fragrant, are mainly in a range from dark crimson through mauve to palest pink or white. However, since the 1900s selective breeding has produced many modern shrub roses with an extended flowering period and in a wider colour range. David Austin's 'English' roses combine shrubby characteristics with a degree of perpetual flowering.

Some shrub roses are vast and spreading, suitable for the larger garden and appropriate for curtaining old trees; these include the species *R. mulliganii*, the famed *R. filipes* 'Kiftsgate', the desirable 'Bobbie James' and 'Rambling Rector' and,

Rosa filipes 'Kiftsgate'

Rosa 'The Garland'

Rosa 'Rambling Rector'

Miss Jekyll's favourite, 'The Garland'. Then there are the healthy suckering roses, which need not be underplanted. Among these are the spring-flowering Scotch burnet roses, varieties and hybrids of *R. pimpinellifolia*, and the American species *RR. virginiana*, *palustris* and *nitida*, which are useful end-of-season performers. Among the bushy Rugosas there are roses of all sizes for mixed companion planting. With apple-green crinkly leaves and carmine, pink or white flowers followed by large red or orange hips, they can be used as garden features, for hedging and, as they are impervious to salt winds, for seaside planting. Some of the Rugosa hybrids, such as the trailing 'Max Graf', are glossy-leaved groundhuggers. Other prostrate roses are the dense and prickly species *R. × paulii* and its pink hybrid 'Paulii Rosea'. 'Raubritter', with dense globular pink flower heads, will clothe banks and suppress weeds.

Personally, even when I am gardening in a small space, I prefer to have a few large shrub roses rather than the more compact and – to me – less graceful varieties. Any garden can find room for the grey-leaved *R. glauca*, which creates little shade and fits in with all mixed planting. Among old roses, Gallicas are the smallest: their gloriously

Rosa 'Complicata'

Rosa sericea ssp. *omeiensis* f. *pteracantha*

shaped and scented flowers make up for their lack of distinction in habit. Another of my favourites is 'Irène Watts' which grows only to 60cm/2ft across. It has peachy-pink flowers opening from pointed buds.

I grew some shrub roses in my first farmhouse garden when I was a complete beginner, choosing those I had liked in other gardens. At Hadspen I extended the range, mixing them with other shrubs. I remember planting the pink-flowered modern shrub *R.* 'Complicata' to grow through quick-growing sea buckthorn, *Hippophaë rhamnoides*, later adding blue-flowered *Clematis* 'Perle d'Azur' to clamber between the grey leaves of the upper branches of the buckthorn for late-summer effects, and underplanting the scheme with *Geranium* × *oxonianum* 'Wargrave Pink'. Elsewhere I experimented with roses interesting for their foliage, bark or translucent thorns. *R. omeiensis*, now *R. sericea* ssp. *omeiensis*, from the Himalaya, has fern-like foliage and stout branches armed with bright translucent red thorns. *R.s.* ssp. *omeiensis* f. *pteracantha* has brown stems clad with wedge-shaped thorns. The smaller *R. primula* has brown thorny stems and fern-like leaves. *R. roxburghii*, the burr or chestnut rose, which thrives in the southern states of America, is distinct, with tawny-brown slightly angular stems and flaky bark. The flowers are shell-pink.

At Tintinhull we have massed beds of the old apothecary's rose, *R. gallica* var. *officinalis*, at the south end of the Kitchen Garden, and the grey-leaved *R.* 'Wolley-Dod' (*R. villosa* 'Duplex'), grows as a towering hedge at the north end. We have the true *R. villosa* (*R. pomifera*) at the edge of the eastern pathway, with *R. nutkana*

'Plena', *R.* 'Geranium' and the Damask rose 'Ispahan' nearby. We also grow both old and modern shrub roses as companion plants scattered throughout all the borders in the garden. With few exceptions we stick to scented roses with a traditional colour range.

Unless you are a collector, the shrub roses in your garden must be easy to manage, healthy and vigorous. Rose replant disease is a recurring problem in many gardens, including Tintinhull. When we first came we had to sterilize or replace the soil wherever there had been roses or members of the Rosaceae family (see page 207). If your garden is similarly affected you may need to do the same, or, alternatively, not grow roses in that part of the garden for at least five years.

Shrub roses, old and new, like rich feeding with organic mulches. Generally, little pruning is needed, but if necessary whole branches can be cut back after

flowering and in winter the oldest wood can be cut to ground level, opening out the centre of the bush. Any frost-tipped shoots should be removed in early spring. You can avoid the chore of removing suckers by growing the roses on their own roots (see page 111). These roses should never be sheared off at a uniform height to make a frill of new growth. It is their graceful habit, as much as their flowering beauty, which makes them such an asset in the garden.

Rosa 'Ispahan'

Hardy Geraniums

When I began to garden, my first 'scheme' was a small collection of shrub roses underplanted with crane's-bill geraniums. The twining stems, thick foliage and gentle flowing habits of geraniums seemed to make them especially suitable for growing around the base of bare rugged rose stems. The flower colours, also, in misty blues, dark velvet-purple and brighter pinks and magentas, often enlivened by deeper veining, seemed to tone successfully with all the shrub roses I had. From that day, I have valued their many qualities.

There are hardy geraniums to suit most

Geranium pratense 'Plenum Violaceum'

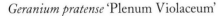

Geranium maderense

situations. They are invaluable for infilling between more disciplined upright plants, happily weaving their way to cover the soil. None seem fussy about the soil type but most show some preference between sun or shade and dry or moist situations. Some, including *Geranium cinereum*, *G. macrorrhizum*, *G. phaeum*, *G. platypetalum*, *G. clarkei* 'Kashmir White' and 'Kashmir Purple', *G. pratense* 'Plenum Violaceum', *G. renardii* and *G. sylvaticum*, make wide hummocks. A few, such as *G. psilostemon*, with black-centred magenta flowers and

autumn-tinted foliage, grow more upright. A third category is tender and includes two stars, the self-seeding *G. maderense* and *G. palmatum*. Both are handsome foliage plants with clusters of pink-mauve flowers. The taller *G. palmatum* is most ornamental and is good for containers; *G. maderense* seeds prolifically at Tintinhull, surviving in sheltered corners through all but the hardest winters.

The geraniums most commonly grown are violet-blue *G. × magnificum*, *G. × oxonianum* and its hybrids and cultivars (the

On pages 118-19, left to right:
Geranium phaeum
Geranium clarkei 'Kashmir White'
Geranium pratense 'Mrs Kendall Clark'

very vigorous *G. × o.* 'Claridge Druce', with grey-green leaves and magenta-pink flowers, and *G. × o.* 'Wargrave Pink', with brighter pink petals than the type) and forms of the much lower-growing smaller magenta *G. sanguineum*. Of these I like best 'Glenluce', with clear pink flowers, which I use as a carpet under pink roses.

My favourites – for the veined beauty of their flowers and their natural habit – are varieties of *G. pratense*, the meadow crane's-bill. As their name suggests, they prefer open, field-like conditions. *G. pratense* itself is tall and graceful, increasing around the garden by self-sown seed. Good varieties include *G.p.* 'Striatum', with veined petals, and *G.p.* 'Mrs Kendall Clark', with pearly-grey flowers. The double forms with rosette-like flowers are most compact for border grouping; both lavender-blue *G.p.* 'Plenum Caeruleum' and the richer violet-blue *G.p.* 'Plenum Violaceum' make long-flowering companions for strong perennials. Two varieties of *G. clarkei*, 'Kashmir Purple' and 'Kashmir White', have many of the *pratense* characteristics, but, spreading by rhizomes, are lower-growing.

I particularly admire those geraniums which really prefer shade; so much the better if they will also tolerate dry conditions. The European *G. nodosum* grows to 45cm/18in, with glossy leaves and small lilac flowers; it self-seeds under evergreens, its flowers paling if in full sun. Equally tolerant of shade is *G. phaeum*, the mourning widow, with small dark maroon, almost black, flowers; its white variety is even more desirable.

Geranium phaeum 'Album'

A Wealth of Viburnums

Viburnum × *carlcephalum*

Evergreen and deciduous viburnums are among the best and most versatile of shrubs, with beautiful white or pink-flushed flowers, good black, red or turquoise fruits (provided there is the necessary cross-pollination) and, in many cases, striking autumn foliage. There are winter-, spring- and autumn-flowering viburnums, and there are many cultivars suitable for the smaller garden.

Growing in sun or semi-shade, viburnums like moist conditions. They enjoy a rich loamy soil but are not at all fussy about whether it is acid or alkaline. Pruning consists of removing old or dead wood in spring, at the same time carefully cutting back any of the evergreen varieties which take up more than their allotted space. They can be propagated from late-summer cuttings of semi-ripe wood. All deciduous viburnums allow small bulbs and little woodlanders to grow under their skirts, while the bushier evergreens can be trained against walls to save space.

Deciduous viburnums

In autumn and early winter, and continuously in mild spells through the succeeding few months, the remarkably frost-resistant rose-tinted flowers of the deciduous *Viburnum farreri* waft their scent through the garden. The hybrid *V.* × *bodnantense* 'Dawn' also flowers from late autumn to early spring, its rich rose-red buds opening on the leafless stem to white flushed with pink. *V. carlesii*, its many garden cultivars and its hybrid *V.* × *carlcephalum* all flower in early spring. All are pink-budded, fragrant, medium-sized and compact, and can be trained to make round-headed standards.

V. sargentii 'Onondaga', with maple-like leaves, bronze when young and again in autumn, flowers early. It is a compact bush for the smaller garden. When space is not a problem, forms of the guelder rose, *V. opulus*, are highly desirable. The sterile cultivar with creamy snowball flowers *V.o.* 'Roseum' (*V.o.* 'Sterile') is wonderful

in late spring, and the yellow-fruited *V.o.* 'Xanthocarpum' is decorative later.

Perhaps the loveliest form of the prized Japanese snowball, *V. plicatum*, is *V.p.* 'Mariesii', with tabulated branches bearing white lacecap flowers. The foliage colours well for the late summer. It is an architectural shrub to be paired for corners or used singly as a focal point. A smaller version, *V.p.* 'Nanum Semperflorens' (*V.p.* 'Watanabe'), grows slowly into an almost conical shape. *V.p.* 'Grandiflorum' has large white sterile flower heads.

Both *V. dilatatum* and the lofty *V. betulifolium* would be worth growing for their clusters of redcurrant-like fruit alone, but these are large shrubs, more suitable for woodland. To ensure cross-pollination, several, from different sources, should be grown in a group. An American hybrid of *V. dilatatum*, *V.* 'Oneida', grows to 3m/10ft only, and has creamy-white flower trusses and dark glossy leaves.

Evergreens

Forms of the evergreen laurustinus, *Viburnum tinus*, are robust winter-flowering shrubs. They have a dense bushy habit and are clothed to the ground with glossy green leaves, which makes them suitable for hedging. Their pink-budded flat white flowers are followed by metallic blue fruit.

Viburnum × *bodnantense* 'Dawn'

Viburnum plicatum 'Mariesii'

Viburnum × burkwoodii

Viburnum tinus 'Eve Price'

I prefer the more compact cultivar 'Eve Price', with attractive flattened heads of carmine buds and pink-tinged flowers.

V. × *burkwoodii* is one of my favourite viburnums. With leaves shining above but brownish-felted beneath, it produces scented pink-budded flowers from midwinter until late spring. For very cold areas, *V.* 'Pragense', bred in Prague and adapted to a continental climate, is an alternative; neither leaves nor buds are ever damaged by frost. *V. rhytidophyllum* is another useful plant which will thrive in a cold garden; it will also tolerate chalk. *V. henryi* is not often seen, but it is a handsome open shrub with narrow glossy green leaves and fragrant white flower panicles in early summer. *V.* × *hillieri* 'Winton' is semi-evergreen and bears masses of creamy-white flower panicles in midsummer. Also summer-flowering, and very attractive, are *V. cinnamomifolium*, with interesting reddish stalks to the leaves, and *V. cylindricum*, which has leaves with a waxy metallic sheen.

On a spring day at dawn in the Pool Garden, trees from behind the walls are reflected in the central pool. Beside the summerhouse the acid-yellow of the large euphorbias contrasts with the differing blues of ceanothus and spiky *Iris pallida* ssp. *pallida*. The flag iris, *Iris pseudacorus*, in the water, can spread at an alarming rate, but its leaves and flowers unify the scheme.

THE POOL GARDEN

ALTHOUGH THE Pool Garden is hidden away in the centre of the garden complex, direct axes and cross views to other garden sections unite it with the design as a whole. Screened from other areas by tall yew hedges on either side, it has a classical rectangular layout. The plan is simple, and the volume of space created by symmetrically arranged lawns and water, by vertical walls of yew and by the sky overhead, harks back to the enclosed Muslim garden and the Italian Renaissance garden which derived from it.

Until 1947 the whole Pool Garden space, enclosed on the east and west by yew hedges and on the north by a wall, was a tennis court. Mrs Reiss raised £500 by the sale of an old cider orchard across the road and used the money to lay out the canal with its flanking grass panels and the main borders and to build the summerhouse. She dedicated this new garden area to the memory of her nephew, a pilot killed in the last year of the 1939–45 war.

In fact the area is not an exact rectangle but its irregularities, including a definite slant to the south, are disguised by clever planting. Mrs Reiss gave the pool and summerhouse central positions and made the flower beds flanking the summerhouse asymmetrical. This adjustment, although of minimal necessity here, is worth remembering, for the principle can be applied to any awkwardly shaped site. If the dominant features of the garden space are centred and aligned, the eye will overlook irregularities, perhaps in awkward perimeter lines, and will automatically home in on the geometry. It is surprising how many seemingly formal gardens are made in shapes that are not symmetrical and do not have straight edges. In some, particularly the linear gardens made by the French in the seventeenth century, the laws of perspective controlled distance and size, and plants were deliberately set closer together or further apart to create definite effects. The same rules of vision can be applied to planting and, in conjunction with the principles of colour theory, they can be used to deceive the eye and make a satisfactorily balanced picture.

The summerhouse in the Pool Garden, with its view down the formal pool to the urn in the Middle Garden, is the natural centre of the whole garden at Tintinhull. All routes around the garden lead to it. Seats are placed invitingly in the shady interior, and decorative pots, filled with exotic or fragrant plants, are arranged to give

Left: The Pool Garden at midday, looking south, with the Middle Garden's tall spreading holm oaks reflected in the pool. All still-water schemes should be managed so that at least two-thirds of the water surface is kept clear of aquatics. In the end borders, part of the Middle Garden scheme, the variegated elder and the pyracantha are in full flower.

Right: On the corner of the summerhouse, the dark purple flowers of Clematis *Jackmanii Superba' entangle with bronze-leaved* Vitis vinifera *'Purpurea'. Regale lilies, blue salvias and white argyranthemums grow in the pots just in front of the building.*

pleasure. From here the distinctive colour schemes of the two contrasting main borders in the Pool Garden can be viewed and appraised simultaneously.

The Pool Garden's rigid architectural layout is interlaced with loose organic planting. Small trees, shrubs and soft-stemmed plants growing in naturalistic profusion overlap the stiff lines of walls, hedges and front border edges. Hedge-clipping, mowing and edge-trimming are done by rule, but the management of the free-style planting is more demanding. It requires a good knowledge of the plants' behaviour and needs, as well as a trained eye for proportion and colour. This is what might be called 'skilled' rather than 'high' maintenance. It is the sort of gardening challenge that I enjoy and often suggest to clients.

Each of the two main borders has a break in the centre. In one a seat is framed by plain yew; the other reveals the archway over the steps which descend to the Kitchen Garden and the rose walk. Both colour schemes are typically Tintinhull in style but, as in any mixed border, the shapes of plants and the colours and textures of leaves play an important supporting role. The border scheme on the west side of the garden has strong and bright colours, a 'hot' mixture; the eastern borders are planted with groups of predominantly pale-coloured 'cool' flowerers. Both schemes are planned to reach a peak from mid- to late summer, but both include a few spring-flowering shrubs – *Cytisus* × *praecox* and a smoke bush in the hot borders, deutzias and *Viburnum plicatum* 'Mariesii' in the pale borders, philadelphus in both.

Although the Pool Garden is self-consciously designed for colour patterns and repetitions, a more naturalistic spirit is introduced, as in all the other Tintinhull 'rooms', by encouraging a certain amount of spontaneous seeding. In the hot borders soaring verbascums establish in both the back and the front of the beds, while in the paler composition grey-leaved opium poppies seed in drifts between established clumps of perennials.

The main colour impact begins in June, when the defined colour schemes become recognizable. Throughout the summer, plants in containers – at the corners of the pool, in and outside the summerhouse, on steps and in the alcove of yew at the south end of the hot borders – bulk up the adjacent border colour schemes. Green leaves in different textures and sizes and more self-consciously placed grey and silver foliage plants, laced through both schemes, link and integrate the borders, bringing out the paler hues and exaggerating the more vivid. Although planted as naturally as possible, with tightly packed colour drifts interweaving to blur sharp-edged divisions, these beds are the most 'dressed' in the garden. At summer's peak the pale west-facing borders are most spectacular in the early morning mists; the scheme opposite is mellowed and rich in evening light, as shadows lengthen and the sun drops below the high hedge.

Above: *Chocolate-scented* Cosmos atrosanguineus *grows in terracotta pots by the stone bench in the south-west corner of the Pool Garden, beside an annual cuphea. This cosmos is quite hardy if protectively mulched during the winter months, but as it comes through the soil very late I prefer to keep it safe in pots.*

Opposite: *A corner of the Pool Garden, looking especially romantic in the early morning light. Tumbling lady's mantle (Alchemilla mollis) covers the ground beneath large-leaved Crambe cordifolia, while a vertical yellow-flowered verbascum and a self-seeded Eryngium giganteum contribute their contrasting flower and leaf textures. Scarlet 'Frensham' roses in the background give a hint of the hot colours which are the main theme of this border.*

The Hot Borders

T HE WESTERN BORDERS are primarily intended to convey strong colour sensations. As you turn to face them, hot colours blast the retina and compel a second or two of refocusing, especially after the eye has become accustomed to the softly tinted colours of the pale beds. Scarlet, vermilion and crimson reds, with yellows and oranges, all from one segment of the colour wheel, assail the perception; even the pockets of gentle silvery foliage, mainly senecios (now *Brachyglottis* 'Sunshine') and *Artemisia* 'Powis Castle', although allowing some relief, by contrast make the strong neighbouring hues even more arresting.

When we came to Tintinhull in the winter of 1979–80 these borders had been half-emptied in preparation for soil sterilization, mainly against replant diseases. In spring we removed the rest of the plants, storing many through the summer for replanting in the following autumn and spring. The plans for the replanting scheme, which we implemented, were drawn up by Jim Marshall, the National Trust Gardens' Adviser who had taken over responsibility for Tintinhull in the previous year. Mrs Reiss left no planting plans or even plant lists for these borders, and Jim's drawings were mainly based on what we had found still in the beds and on photographs showing red 'Frensham' roses, blue delphiniums and bright yellow achilleas. The roses were planted in four repetitive clumps (two clumps of three in each bed). Jim also put in green-leaved smoke bushes (one in each border – one has since died) and two groups of shrubby variegated snowberries. He used *Potentilla* 'Gibson's Scarlet' and tall orange tiger lilies, both of which have been a huge success. Red dahlias were to be added each year.

Like all detailed plans which include a mixture of shrubs and perennials, these blueprints were only a start. Each season since then, usually in spring, we move groups about to get relationships

I particularly enjoy the view looking along the red and yellow border. By our later years at Tintinhull the midsummer colouring was less hot than it had been earlier, when we had more orange and red flowers. Last summer, when this photograph was taken, the brilliant red of the 'Frensham' roses mingled with the pale blooms of Clematis recta, Nectaroscordum siculum *ssp.* bulgaricum, Lilium regale, Aruncus dioicus *'Kneiffii' and* Verbascum *'Vernale', the dark purple foliage of* Lysimachia ciliata *'Purpurea' and the yellow-edged leaves of* Symphoricarpos orbiculatus *'Foliis Variegatis'.*

Tall verbascums and crambes, Alchemilla mollis *and 'Frensham' roses thrive around the armillary sphere in the central division of the hot borders. The background frame of the dark green yew hedge and the classical ornament give definition to the luxuriant cottage-style planting.*

right and try new combinations. At first we used only plants recommended to us by the Trust but gradually we became more adventurous, trying suitable new plants and giving up those which failed to get the effects we wanted and believed Mrs Reiss had striven for. The Trust had already replaced *Artemisia absinthium* 'Lambrook Silver' with the bushy *A.* 'Powis Castle', not in existence during Mrs Reiss's time. In breaking with tradition by using a 'new' plant they set a precedent for our experimentation over the next years. (Recently in the United States I met an even more interesting form, *A. absinthium* 'Huntington Gardens', with more distinguished habit, but I have not yet been able to find it in Britain.) We planted delphiniums behind the red roses, as she had done, but Jim must have chosen the wrong shade of blue. For three years we cut off their flower heads as they came into bloom, finding their contrast with the roses too acute. A more purple blue, with some red in it, might have been more successful.

To the 1981 plans we have added scarlet *Crocosmia* 'Lucifer' and some of the bronze-leaved lobelias such as *Lobelia* 'Dark Crusader' (we dig this up in autumn, in spring divide it in containers, and

replant it in early May). More recently we have put in the perennial purple-leaved *Lysimachia ciliata* 'Purpurea'; with its small yellow flowers nestling between the coloured leaves, and a spreading habit, it is perfect for the scheme. At first, as recommended by the Trust, we used red penstemons, grown annually from cuttings and overwintered in cold frames, to bulk up the front of the beds. *Penstemon hartwegii* and *P.* 'Garnet', both dark red, as well as the more vivid 'Scarlet Fire', fitted exactly into the colour harmonies. However, in one hard winter we lost all our cuttings and the following summer we used scarlet tobacco flowers instead, planting four strong clumps of *Nicotiana* 'Scarlet Bedder' along the front of the beds. The next year we substituted tender woody red salvias, which I prefer; but for this scheme it is important to choose those with clear or dark red flowers, avoiding the more cherry hues. *Salvia fulgens*, *S. coccinea* and *S. elegans* all work well (they are useful in the middle of the border as well as along the front edge). More recently we have used red and yellow figwort (*Phygelius*) from South Africa to get our foreground effects. I first admired groups of red- and yellow-flowered forms at the Cambridge Botanic Garden and, as we seemed to be getting hotter and drier summers, decided to attempt a similar combination. *Phygelius × rectus* 'African Queen' and *P. aequalis* 'Yellow Trumpet' now make suckering groups.

The 'Frensham' roses remain a mainstay of the whole border, particularly spectacular in June, but blooming in bursts throughout the rest of the summer. There are few late-flowering red shrubs or perennials to take over when 'Frensham' leaves off, so annuals and tender shrubby plants such as the salvias (overwintered as rooted cuttings) are important to keep the scheme going. We often use dahlias such as 'Bishop of Llandaff' and 'Bloodstone' which fill in during the latter half of the season. We have few yellows and oranges in the early months of summer but many Compositae contribute later. Daisy-flowered achilleas, rudbeckias and bigeneric × *Solidaster hybridus* are essentials, but we avoid the more bronze-flowered heleniums. Creams are also easy to find and we use more of these than in Mrs Reiss's time, softening some of her brightest colour associations. A tall bushy broom, *Cytisus × praecox*, flowers early, quickly followed by cream-flowered camassias which tend to seed throughout, as also does *Nectaroscordum siculum* ssp. *bulgaricum*. Corner plants of architectural *Crambe cordifolia* have wide umbels of small white flowers rising above massive heart-shaped green leaves, to make a statement by the end of May. A large group of cream-coloured *Clematis recta* opens beside tall glaucous-leaved thalictrum (*Thalictrum flavum* ssp. *glaucum*). *Achillea filipendulina* 'Gold Plate' has flat heads of harsh yellow; if I were to follow my own preference, I would replace this with one of the paler cultivars. Red-hot pokers – an unnamed variety we found here – and tall mulleins (*Verbascum* 'Vernale'), allowed to seed through the two beds, make vertical accents. *Crocosmia* 'Lucifer' is a shaft of scarlet in late summer. If there is any space we add groups of *Nicotiana langsdorffii* and *Argyranthemum* 'Jamaica Primrose', which fit equally appropriately into the opposite cool scheme. We have also encouraged orange- and red-flowered forms of *Eccremocarpus scaber* and the yellow canary creeper (*Tropaeolum peregrinum*) to seed freely and twine among shrubs and perennials to further extend the colour scheme.

Over the years we have experimented with colour sequences, finding it best to repeat each vivid hue at least once within the range of vision, but also striving to blend in the same progression colours which are adjacent to each other on the colour wheel. Drifts of pale cream and primrose next to brighter buttercup, then oranges, then scarlets and so on to deeper reds and crimson.

Above: *Like most loosestrifes,* Lysimachia ciliata *'Purpurea' is a rapid colonizer. This cultivar is splendid beneath the 'Frensham' roses, its purple leaves and pale yellow flowers their perfect complement.*

Below: *The tall* Reseda luteola *has pale yellow spikes which seem just right as an addition to the stronger oranges, yellows and reds. It grows to 1.5–1.8m/5–6ft but needs no staking. We hope that it will self-seed with the years and fill in any bare patches of soil.*

Lobelia
'Dark Crusader'

Crocosmia masoniorum

Lilium henryi

Crocosmia 'Lucifer'

Sisyrinchium striatum

Cotinus coggygria

Heuchera micrantha
'Palace Purple'

Self seeders
Achemilla mollis
Camassia
Eccremocarpus scaber
Eryngium giganteum
Euphorbia stricta
Nectaroscordum siculum
  spp. bulgaricum
Oenothera biennis
Sisyrinchium striatum
Tropaeolum peregrinum
Verbascum 'Vernale'

SUMMMER PLANTING

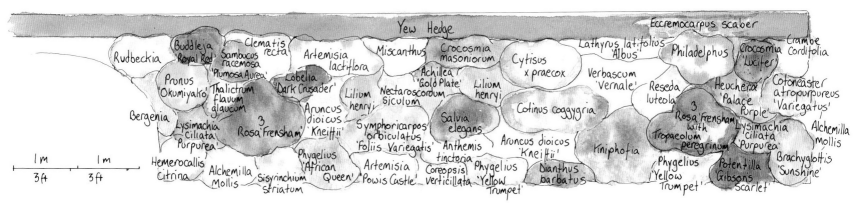

Yew Hedge — Eccremocarpus scaber

Rudbeckia · Buddleja 'Royal Red' · Clematis recta · Sambucus racemosa 'Plumosa Aurea' · Artemisia lactiflora · Miscanthus · Crocosmia masoniorum · Cytisus x praecox · Lathyrus latifolius 'Albus' · Philadelphus · Crocosmia 'Lucifer' · Crambe cordifolia · Prunus 'Okumiyako' · Thalictrum flavum glaucum · Lobelia 'Dark Crusader' · Lilium henryi · Nectaroscordum siculum · Achillea 'Gold Plate' · Lilium henryi · Verbascum 'Vernale' · Reseda luteola · Heuchera 'Palace Purple' · Cotoneaster atropurpureus 'Variegatus' · Bergenia · Lysimachia Ciliata Purpurea · 3 Rosa 'Frensham' · Aruncus dioicus 'Kneiffii' · Symphoricarpos orbiculatus 'Foliis Variegatis' · Salvia elegans · Cotinus coggygria · 3 Rosa 'Frensham' with Tropaeolum peregrinum · Lysimachia Ciliata Purpurea · Alchemilla mollis · Hemerocallis Citrina · Alchemilla Mollis · Sisyrinchium striatum · Phygelius 'African Queen' · Artemisia 'Powis Castle' · Anthemis tinctoria · Coreopsis verticillata · Phygelius 'Yellow Trumpet' · Aruncus dioicus 'Kneiffii' · Dianthus barbatus · Kniphofia · Phygelius 'Yellow Trumpet' · Potentilla 'Gibsons scarlet' · Brachyglottis 'Sunshine'

1m / 3ft   1m / 3ft

Alchemilla mollis and
Brachyglottis 'Sunshine'

Salvia fulgens

Nectaroscordum siculum ssp. bulgaricum

Nicotiana
langsdorffii

Rosa 'Frensham'

× Solidaster hybridus

Phygelius × rectus
'African Queen'

→ N

Yew Hedge

Crambe corditolia — Miscanthus sinensis 'Variegatus' — Eryngium giganteum — Artemisia lactiflora — Cytisus × praecox — Crambe corditolia — Clematis recta — Buddleja 'Royal Red' — Nectaroscordum siculum — Clematis 'Huldine'

Alchemilla mollis — Armillary sphere — Eryngium giganteum — 3 Rosa 'Frensham' — Rosa moyesii — Verbascum 'vernale' — Crocosmia — Salvia fulgens — Thalictrum flavum glaucum — Laburnum × watereri 'Vossii' — Lysimachia ciliata 'Purpurea'

Crambe corditolia — Lilium lancifolium fortunei — Lysimachia ciliata 'Purpurea' — Lobelia 'Dark Crusader' — Achillea 'Gold Plate' — Lilium lancifolium fortunei — 3 Rosa 'Frensham' — Alchemilla Mollis — Taxus baccata 'Dovastonii Aurea'

Brachyglottis 'Sunshine' — Phygelius 'Yellow Trumpet' — Artemisia 'Powis Castle' — Nicotiana langsdorffii — × Solidaster hybridus — Symphoricarpos orbiculatus 'Foliis Variegatis' — Salvia coccinea — Nicotiana langsdorffii — Coreopsis verticillata — Artemisia 'Powis Castle' — Phygelius 'Yellow Trumpet'

Verbascum 'vernale' — Phygelius 'African Queen'

The Pale Borders

There is a much greater choice of plants suitable for the beds with cooler colours, and here, rather than colour harmonies based on a narrow segment of the spectrum as in the west border, we have more definite associations and repetitions, with colours taken from a wider range. Indeed, there are so many perennials to choose from that selection and repetition is the key; without this the whole scheme would collapse into bland chaos. Interestingly, over the years, as we have fiddled with the planting in this area, we have gradually eliminated all yellows except for thalictrum and cephalaria, both of which flower in early summer before the main purpose of the border scheme becomes apparent, and *Argyranthemum* 'Jamaica Primrose' for late-summer performance; all of these have very pale flower colour. Blues, mauves, pinks and some creamy whites are now the predominant colours, with tones of blue used more frequently than any other. This reflects my own preferences for harmonies.

Without strong, eye-catching hues, the success of the overall design depends on unity of purpose. Each colour group, usually but not always of the same plant, is repeated either twice in the length of the two sections which comprise the border or twice in one of the sections. In early summer clumps of brilliant blue *Galega orientalis* flower at opposite ends of the two beds, while ordinary bicoloured goat's rue, *G. officinalis*, flowering a few weeks later, has a more central position. White-flowered epilobium (*Epilobium angustifolium album*) appears both near the centre and closer to the southern end. A pair of white Rugosa roses, *Rosa* 'Blanche Double de Coubert', underplanted with glossy-leaved *Acanthus mollis latifolius* and *Polemonium* 'Lambrook Mauve', frames the seat between the beds. Clumps of pink and mauve phlox are distributed in less formal fashion throughout both sections. White and cream flowerers are the white mugwort (*Artemisia lactiflora*), blackroot (*Veronicastrum virginicum album*) and a bugbane, the snakeroot (*Cimicifuga racemosa*), all with interesting foliage which contributes from early in the season. Groups of violet-blue *Salvia nemorosa* 'Lubecca' give a darker tone.

Although the scheme is by no means a formal pattern, many similar plant drifts and clumps touch and weave together to give an impression of unity. There are clumps of pale blue aster (*Aster × frikartii* 'Mönch') and low-growing pink diascias – a South African plant revelling in hot sun – almost symmetrically placed along the front edge. These, together with silver-leaved artemisias and the

Above: *The uncommon apricot-flowered* Collomia grandiflora *groups itself in early summer in front of* Erysimum *'Bowles' Mauve'. This collomia, acquired by accident, is a self-seeder and an invaluable addition to the pale borders.*

Right: *In my last summer at Tintinhull all the perennials and annuals were newly planted in the pale borders. Bright carmine* Silene armeria, *opium poppies, silvery* Artemisia *'Powis Castle', white epilobiums and felicias give quick seasonal effects in a new planting scheme.*

dark yew hedge, hold the design together through the long season. Perhaps all this sounds rather too carefully arranged, but informal notes are sounded with annual opium poppies, peony-flowered in pink and mauve, encouraged to seed in drifts between flower groups. Another annual seeder, the little known *Collomia grandiflora* from western North America, with distinct apricot flowers, also seeds *in situ* at one end, while *Silene armeria* with bright pink flowers and glaucous leaves spreads at the other. Each year the tiny knotweed, *Polygonum capitatum*, germinates between the cracks along the stone edging in front of the beds. Encouraging these annual effects with self-seeders is a very personal way of gardening.

These eastern borders were completely emptied in the autumn of 1981. They were replanted, after the soil had been sterilized, in the spring of 1982. In 1992–3 they were again redone. Because of this disturbance – all the perennials were stored in the Kitchen Garden

Left: Deutzia setchuenensis, *the last of the deutzias to flower at Tintinhull, produces its innumerable white star-like blossoms in July and August. This deutzia is reputedly not entirely hardy, but the Tintinhull plant never seems to be affected by severe winters.*

Below left: *The pinkish-blues of goat's rue,* Galega officinalis, *fit perfectly into the pale border theme. The earlier-flowering G.* orientalis, *which has dark blue flower spikes and is more of a spreader, also plays an important role in these borders.*

Opposite: *The fireweed,* Epilobium angustifolium album, *with white flowers opening from green-tinged calyces, is one of my favourite perennials. Later in the year the epilobium's seedheads, the seeds enclosed in 'cottonwool', are almost as attractive as the flowers, and last for many weeks. Although this plant does spread – by creeping rootstock – seed seldom germinates, so it is not too difficult to control.*

from early autumn until spring – during 1993 we had to use more annuals and tender plants than usual to bulk up the newly replanted groups of perennials. *Gaura lindheimeri* (a perennial but treated as an annual here), blue-flowered salvias and felicias and mauve *Penstemon venustus* all contributed to the picture.

The appearance of the whole plant or each group of plants throughout the growing season is almost as important as the flower power which is, at best, only fleeting; and in both the east and the west borders plants are chosen for their foliage as well as their flowers. In the hot borders *Crambe cordifolia*, the giant sea kale with umbels of tiny white flowers, is grown for its architectural habit and huge heart-shaped leaves. It is matched by the smaller but equally valuable glossy-leaved *Acanthus mollis latifolius* in the pale borders. Eryngiums have an almost metallic sheen to the leaves. Some vigorous growers, such as the giant crambe, need constant manicuring, with dying leaves removed almost on a daily basis.

Although the hot borders are described as mainly red and yellow, cream flowers and grey foliage are important ingredients, and these are repeated in the cool beds opposite. In the early years we opened our season in April with swathes of dark tulips, 'Queen of Night' in the west beds and pink 'Queen of Bartigons' in those to the east, to give a hint of the themes planned for summer. More recently we have abandoned any early bulbs but allow the mixed greens and textures of emerging perennials, framed by a few early-flowering shrubs, to give us a quieter pleasure.

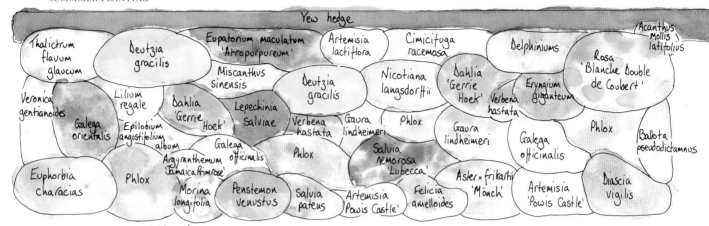

Yew hedge

Thalictrum flavum glaucum

Deutzia gracilis

Eupatorium maculatum 'Atropurpureum'

Artemisia lactiflora

Cimicifuga racemosa

Delphiniums

Acanthus Mollis latifolius

Rosa 'Blanche Double de Coubert'

Veronica gentianoides

Lilium regale

Dahlia 'Gerrie Hoek'

Miscanthus sinensis

Lepechinia Salviae

Deutzia gracilis

Nicotiana langsdorffii

Dahlia 'Gerrie Hoek'

Verbena hastata

Eryngium giganteum

Galega orientalis

Epilobium angostifolium album

Verbena hastata

Gaura lindheimeri

Phlox

Gaura lindheimeri

Phlox

Ballota pseudodictamnus

Galega officinalis

Phlox

Salvia nemorosa 'Lubecca'

Galega officinalis

Euphorbia characias

Phlox

Argyranthemum 'Jamaica Primrose'

Morina longifolia

Penstemon venustus

Salvia patens

Artemisia 'Powis Castle'

Felicia amelloides

Aster × frikartii 'Mönch'

Artemisia 'Powis Castle'

Diascia vigilis

1m
3ft

1m
3ft

Self-seeders
Collomia grandiflora
Eryngium giganteum
Lathyrus vernus
Papaver somniferum
Polygonum capitatum
Silene armeria
Viola 'Bowles' Black'
Viola riviniana Purpurea Group
Viola sororia 'Freckles'
Verbascum 'Vernale'

Lilium regale

Argyranthemum 'Jamaica Primrose'

Verbena hastata

Cimicifuga racemosa

Eryngium giganteum

Felicia amelloides

Phlox paniculata 'Franz Schubert'

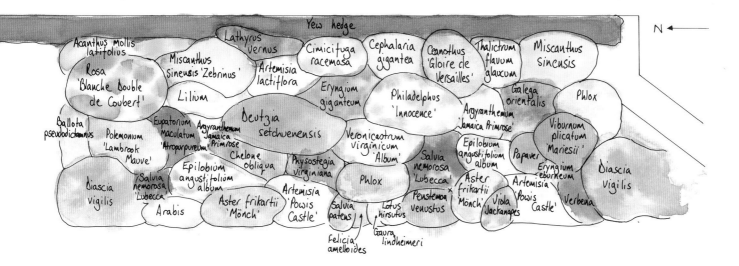

Yew hedge

N

Acanthus mollis latifolius
Rosa 'Blanche Double de Coubert'
Lathyrus vernus
Miscanthus Sinensis 'Zebrinus'
Artemisia lactiflora
Cimicifuga racemosa
Cephalaria gigantea
Ceanothus 'Gloire de Versailles'
Thalictrum flavum glaucum
Miscanthus sinensis
Lilium
Eryngium giganteum
Philadelphus 'Innocence'
Galega orientalis
Phlox
Ballota pseudodictamnus
Eupatorium maculatum 'Atropurpureum'
Polemonium 'Lambrook Mauve'
Argyranthemum 'Jamaica Primrose'
Deutzia setchuenensis
Veronicastrum virginicum 'Album'
Argyranthemum 'Jamaica Primrose'
Viburnum plicatum 'Mariesii'
Chelone obliqua
Physostegia virginiana
Epilobium angustifolium album
Papaver
Eryngium eburneum
Diascia vigilis
Diascia vigilis
Salvia nemorosa 'Lubecca'
Epilobium angustifolium album
Phlox
Salvia nemorosa 'Lubecca'
Aster frikartii 'Mönch'
Artemisia 'Powis Castle'
Verbena
Arabis
Aster frikartii 'Mönch'
Artemisia 'Powis Castle'
Salvia patens
Lotus hirsutus
Penstemon × venustus
Viola 'Jackanapes'
Felicia amelloides
Gaura lindheimeri

Salvia patens

Rosa 'Blanche Double de Coubert'

Physostegia virginiana

Penstemon venustus

Epilobium angustifolium album

Diascia vigilis

Viola 'Jackanapes'

THE SUMMERHOUSE BEDS

THE UNEQUALLY SIZED summerhouse beds that frame the sitting area are backed by stone walls. Climbing pink and red roses, twining clematis, celastrus (*Celastrus orbiculatus* from Asia) and a perennial sweet pea (*Lathyrus rotundifolius*) make a woven background to plants chosen to take the scheme through all the months of the year. Evergreen *Osmanthus heterophyllus*, with glossy holly-like leaves, and the broad shape of the St Lucie cherry (*Prunus mahaleb*) on one side balance with shining *Piptanthus nepalensis* and a vast *Ceanothus* 'Cascade' on the other. A wide bush of *Phlomis fruticosa* gives protection to emerging clematis shoots. In one or other of the borders, sometimes in both, we grow my favourite Bowles' wallflower (*Erysimum* 'Bowles' Mauve'). If the winter has been kind it will flower for many months in spring, its bushy habit,

grey-green leaves and clear mauve-pink flowers a perpetual joy. We always keep some specimens as a reserve in case of a hard winter. Rooted the previous summer, they are safe in our cold frames. Spring-flowering *Daphne* × *burkwoodii* 'Somerset', with delicate pink buds and fragrance, is almost evergreen, as is the blue-flowered flag iris (*Iris pallida* ssp. *pallida*) – a real blue and not a purple blue – which flowers in May. Clumps of *Salvia officinalis* and the tender

In the western summerhouse border in spring, the tender Euphorbia mellifera *flowers near* Erysimum *'Bowles' Mauve', and scented* Daphne × burkwoodii *'Somerset'. Behind, against the yew hedge, the St Lucie cherry,* Prunus mahaleb, *is also in bloom.*

Euphorbia mellifera (which may well succumb to hard frosts) are grown for their year-round foliage.

In the west summerhouse bed, the wider of the two, a superb spring performance is given by the St Lucie cherry, with myriad small white flowers in early spring, more subdued than the showy Japanese cousins. It spreads its branches above the prized yellow species *Paeonia mlokosewitschii*, with wide yellow papery flowers (followed by scarlet fruit) held on tall stems above glaucous leaves. The tall silver-leaved Moroccan broom, *Cytisus battandieri*, has primrose-coloured tassels smelling deliciously of pineapples. Nearby is another pale yellow flowerer, *Asphodeline lutea*, with grassy foliage. *Parahebe perfoliata*, with pale blue veronica flowers above grey leaves, is almost evergreen, but benefits from being cut to the ground in spring. It is a determined sun-lover, as also are the small rose 'White Pet', with clusters of pink buds opening to white all through the summer (if regularly deadheaded), *Philadelphus* 'Manteau d'Hermine', a small-leaved mock orange, and *Calamintha nepetoides*, with catmint-like aromatic flowers and foliage. Into any empty spaces we fit lower ground-hugging plants such as *Codonopsis clematidea*, *Sedum* 'Ruby Glow', with glaucous leaves, and *Viola*

riviniana Purpurea Group. A sub-shrub, *Cestrum parqui*, has yellow flowers in July and August, smelling musk-like in the evening.

The scrambling *Convolvulus althaeoides* twines its silvery leaves through the roses, producing its pink flowers in later summer, at the same time as *Clematis* 'Huldine' with greenish-white sepals curtains the back wall. In the last few years *Rehmannia elata* from China, with hooded, foxglove-like, mauve flowers, a plant still relatively new in gardens, has looked exotic in front of the climbers. Though it may not survive a cold winter there is no need to worry, for germinated seedlings will appear at the base of the parent in the following spring. As a precaution we usually grow extra plants from seed. *Penstemon venustus*, very similar to 'Sour Grapes', with

The Moroccan broom, Cytisus battandieri, *with silvery foliage and pineapple-scented flowers in late spring, benefits from the protection and reflection of a warm south-facing wall. In the summerhouse west bed the pale cone-shaped yellow flowers contrast admirably with blue iris and penstemons.*

Above: *The double pink rose 'Climbing Shot Silk' is luxuriant against the wall behind the summerhouse east bed in spring. A salmon-coloured perennial sweet pea,* Lathyrus rotundifolius, *twines through its lower branches and unsightly base to give an extended season of flower. Below are blue irises and Jerusalem sage.*

Right: *The iris-like* Sisyrinchium striatum *flowers in the front of the summerhouse border. The pale yellows and creams of the sisyrinchium seem to have the effect of calming harsher tones, while its slender leaves, although on a small scale, lend architectural coherence to this part of the border.*

mauveish-blue flowers which seem to fit into almost any colour scheme, ensures a sequence of flowers through the summer months (it is also a stalwart performer in the pale border theme). Grown from cuttings each year but often surviving *in situ*, it will flower again in summer if deadheaded after its first flush.

The other, narrower, bed on the east side of the summerhouse has very similar planting. In spring the effects are dramatic, with large clumps of *Euphorbia characias* ssp. *wulfenii* 'Lambrook Gold', its swaying stems of heavy-headed acid-yellow bracts showy in front of one of the most graceful and hardy of the evergreen ceanothus, *Ceanothus* 'Cascade'. On the wall, 'Climbing Shot Silk' is the second rose to flower at Tintinhull each year (the yellow Banksian rose on the south wall of the house is usually first). With double shining petals in pale pink, 'Shot Silk' is trained back hard against the wall;

later, *Lathyrus rotundifolius*, a salmon-pink perennial sweet pea, twines around its stems. Small-flowered *Clematis viticella* 'Purpurea Plena Elegans', with overlapping double flowers, smothers the wall in August and September. In a corner the purple-leaved grape vine, *Vitis vinifera* 'Purpurea', pruned to a few buds each spring, will drape itself over the front pediment of the summerhouse, its leaf colours matching the dark flowers of cherry pie, the fragrant heliotrope, growing in pots below for summer display. *Origanum laevigatum* 'Hopleys', with similar flower hue, is under the wall.

Along the front edge of this narrow border, clumps of rose 'White Pet' flower all summer long to match those in the west bed. From mid-June onwards a larger shrub rose, bronze-leaved *Rosa × odorata* 'Mutabilis', has single flowers of pink fading to yellow, next to *Cistus × skanbergii* with clear bright pink papery flowers.

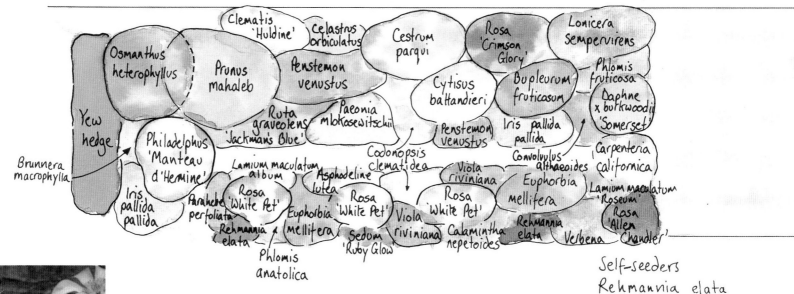

Yew hedge

Osmanthus heterophyllus

Clematis 'Huldine'

Celastrus orbiculatus

Cestrum parqui

Rosa 'Crimson Glory'

Lonicera sempervirens

Prunus mahaleb

Penstemon venustus

Cytisus battandieri

Bupleurum fruticosum

Phlomis fruticosa

Daphne x burkwoodii 'Somerset'

Brunnera macrophylla

Philadelphus 'Manteau d'Hermine'

Ruta graveolens 'Jackman's Blue'

Paeonia mlokosewitschii

Penstemon venustus

Iris pallida pallida

Carpenteria californica

Codonopsis clematidea

Convolvulus althaeoides

Iris pallida pallida

Lamium maculatum album

Asphodeline lutea

Viola riviniana

Euphorbia mellifera

Lamium maculatum 'Roseum'

Bupleurum perfoliatum

Rosa 'White Pet'

Rosa 'White Pet'

Rosa 'White Pet'

Rosa 'Allen Chandler'

Rehmannia elata

Euphorbia mellifera

Viola riviniana

Calamintha nepetoides

Rehmannia elata

Verbena

Phlomis anatolica

Sedum 'Ruby Glow'

Self-seeders
Rehmannia elata
Sisyrinchium striatum

Clematis 'Huldine'

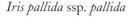

Iris pallida ssp. *pallida*

Paeonia mlokosewitschii

Rehmannia elata

Cytisus battandieri

Carpenteria californica

Rosa 'White Pet'

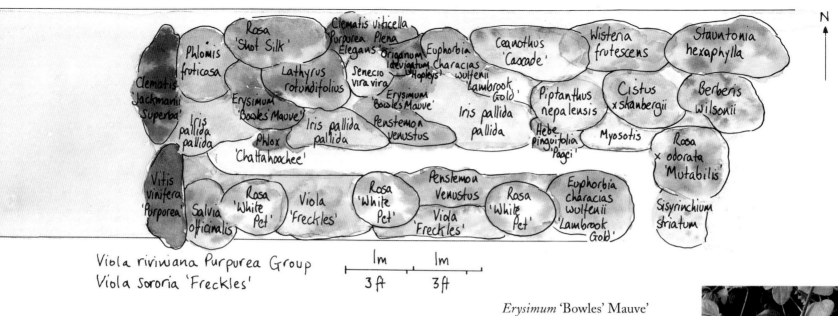

Viola riviniana Purpurea Group
Viola sororia 'Freckles'

1m 1m
3 ft 3 ft

Clematis 'Jackmanii Superba'

Phlomis fruticosa

Erysimum 'Bowles' Mauve'

Clematis viticella
'Purpurea Plena Elegans'

Vitis vinifera 'Purpurea'

Viola sororia 'Freckles'

Phlox 'Chattahoochee'

THE POTS

FOUR LARGE reconstituted stone pots sit on the corners of the pool. We always plant tulips in them for spring: different types with varying times of flowering are planted at different depths to give a longer flowering sequence. We hope they will finish each year just in time for the planting out of annuals, after the last frosts have been predicted, usually about 20 May. We generally concentrate on white and yellow tulips but the lily-flowered 'Burgundy', with deep mauve-purple flowers, has also been a huge success. When flowering is over the bulbs are removed and dried. We do not use them again in the pots but they can be planted elsewhere, for example in the Kitchen Garden where they are grown as cutting flowers. We normally replace the compost in the pots only every three or four years. However, if we have any suspicions of virus we burn the bulbs, scrub out the pots and introduce new compost.

Our summer schemes vary but are similar each year, with plants grown from cuttings and seed. For several years we used centrally placed *Argyranthemum foeniculaceum*, with glaucous leaves and white daisy flowers, surrounded by a mixture of pink nemesias, the little mallow-like *Hibiscus trionum*, with cream maroon-centred flowers, silver helichrysums, and trailing verbenas – both dark blue 'Hidcote Purple' and 'Silver Anne', a pale pink. In the past we have had red-flowered flax (*Linum grandiflorum* 'Rubrum'). *Anisodontea* × *hypomandarum*, from South Africa, is another good centrepiece.

Other decorative pots are arranged in the summerhouse. Some have single specimens such as myrtle or tibouchina, some have a massing of one salvia (*Salvia uliginosa*, *S. patens* or *S. leptophylla*) or the salvia-like *Lepechinia salviae*. Others have mixed summer planting in the same style as the large pots around the pool. The single specimen containers will be removed and replaced as the plants' appearance merits. There is *Trachelospermum jasminoides*, with sweetly scented white flowers, *Melianthus major*, with wide glaucous pinnate leaves, a white-flowered oleander and yellow spring-flowering *Corokia cotoneaster* with wiry stems. But there are many others we have used over the years: daturas

At sunrise in spring, white Tulipa *'Purissima', planted in the pots at the corners of the pool, glows beside the golden-variegated leaves of* Iris pseudacorus. *The early morning light softens the harsh reds and yellows which predominate in the west border later in the season.*

(now brugmansias), other salvias, and sometimes olearias, another favourite genus, most species being too tender for outside wintering at Tintinhull. All the young plants go in one of the greenhouses during the winter. As they get larger they have to survive being in the summerhouse or are abandoned.

In the niche by the stone seat at the end of the west border we have pots of purple-leaved Australian cordylines and phormiums from New Zealand, and yellow- and red-flowered plants picking up the colour scheme of purple, yellow and red in the border. The bright primrose *Calceolaria integrifolia* is grown from cuttings. There are tender cupheas and *Fuchsia* 'Thalia', *Phygelius capensis* 'Winchester Fanfare' and *Bidens* 'Golden Goddess'. These plants, arranged as a picture, are all viewed from the pavement as you enter the garden by the side door. On the opposite side, by the pale border, there are agapanthus in pots, bulked up with silver helichrysums, evolvulus, or any other blue- or pink-flowered annuals available, all colour coordinated with the border planting.

Above left: *In the garden I designed in Michigan, where the summers are very hot, salvias in pots and silver-leaved plants in a majestic urn show planting styles very similar to those used at Tintinhull. In the sunny border behind, eupatoriums and mauve-plumed* Thalictrum rochebrunanum *flourish.*

Left: *The not-altogether-hardy* Salvia uliginosa, *with sky-blue flowers in late summer, seems to perform best when massed in a pot. I have never been so successful with this plant in border schemes and sometimes lose it in a hard winter.*

Opposite: *White daisy-flowered* Argyranthemum foeniculaceum *with glaucous fretted leaves combines with silvery helichrysums and mauve and pink verbenas to sustain summer colour in the main pots around the pool. In the background by the summerhouse, blue* Salvia uliginosa *and silvery* Artemisia arborescens *'Faith Raven', along with plenty of other pot plants, fill this area with flower and foliage interest.*

Planting the Pale Borders

W HEN PLANTING or replanting a border, it is wise to work to a plan, drawn up on graph paper. However, you should always be ready to make changes to planting shapes and quantities as work proceeds.

In the autumn of 1992 we took all the perennials out of the pale borders in preparation for installing a new watering system. Only the shrubs and grasses were left *in situ*. Some of the perennials were stored in trenches in the Kitchen Garden, while others were potted up, after division, in individual pots. The plants we kept in the Kitchen Garden included *Eupatorium maculatum* 'Atropurpureum', salvias such as *Salvia nemorosa* 'Lubecca', and quantities of pink and mauve phlox. We had discarded the central crowns of all these plants, keeping only the younger outer growth. In pots we had, among others, *Polemonium* 'Lambrook Mauve', *Epilobium angustifolium album*, and both sorts of galega, *Galega officinalis*, the ordinary lavender goat's rue, and the dark blue *G. orientalis*.

With the soil in perfect condition – wonderfully friable through having been worked for so many years – the planting began in early April. The bare-rooted plants had to be put in as quickly as possible, before their root systems dried out, so it was particularly important to work in small, easily manageable sections.

I begin any major planting exercise by placing all the plants in position, arranging them in groups, usually of seven or nine plants (*top*). Then I tackle the groups one at a time. To make quite sure the placing stays as I've planned it, before I move a plant to dig its hole I push my trowel in right next to it, to mark its position. Then I quickly dig

the hole and put the plant in – a salvia is shown here – covering the roots with soil and firming the earth down around it (*above and right*).

All potted plants should be given a good soak before planting. The pool at Tintinhull is handy for this, and I 'dunked' all the pots – a pot of *Galega officinalis* is shown (*opposite, above*). If a plant has filled a pot with roots, you may need to scrape the tightly balled roots and compost carefully away from the sides, with your fingers, as you tip it out.

When a whole group has been planted,

I always cover the area with compost, which identifies the newly planted bit, as well as acting as a mulch (*below*).

The planting schemes in the two sections of the pale border refer one to the other, without being strict mirror images. There are more plants in the longer northern section. When planning the replanting I aimed ideally at having at least two groups of each plant throughout the whole scheme. Vigorous spreaders such as *Galega orientalis* were to occupy sites at either end.

When planting or replanting borders in the spring, remember to leave room for any cuttings which may soon be hardy enough to plant out, as well as for any annuals you will wish to include. I put sticks in the middle of each area I wish to reserve for later planting. In the pale borders I left spaces for plants such as diascias and felicias, from the previous year's cuttings, to be massed in groups in the front of both sections of the border, and for two large groups of the pink dahlia 'Gerrie Hoek'. These and other plants grown as annuals would be put out later in the spring. Silvery artemisias, grown from cuttings, would be planted in a formal rhythm along the front of the beds. Alliums and lilies were to be added in the autumn to perform the following year.

Pruning Roses

WHEN PRUNING a rose in late winter or early spring, the aim should be not only to remove old dead, damaged or diseased wood and stimulate new flowering shoots, but also to produce a shapely bush that will make a decorative contribution to the garden even when the plant is not in flower. Make sure you know what kind of rose you are dealing with, though, for Hybrid Teas, Floribundas and other bush roses are treated differently from species roses and large shrubs which, in general, need little spring attention.

The 'Frensham' roses in the Pool Garden's hot borders (*left*) are Floribundas. Grown in a perennial scheme, they strike quite a formal note; but they must be kept well pruned. Our tight packed-in planting style forces even the roses to grow very tall,

and pruning to a good shape is particularly important. However, we do not cut back as hard as is generally advised for Floribundas, because we want the roses to maintain a good height among the other plants in the border.

Though the 'Frenshams' may be trimmed back in autumn or early winter to prevent wind rock, the real pruning is left until early spring, when I start by cutting back any cumbersome top growth with a pruning saw, using the secateurs to hold the branch steady (*left*). Then I remove any weak, dead or diseased stems (*above left*) and cut away about two-thirds of the wood of each branched stem from the previous season. In the case of an old bush that has become congested you may need to cut out the centre in order to allow in light and air.

Some people treat rose-pruning as a work of art, contemplating each cut very deliberately. I prefer to work swiftly towards a final shape that seems to come almost automatically. Using very sharp secateurs,

I make a slanting cut (from which the rain will run off) above an outward-pointing bud, so that subsequent growth does not cause congestion at the centre of the bush (*above centre and right*). I ensure that at least two viable buds remain lower down the branch, and like to leave the bushes at a height of about 60 cm/2ft (*right*).

Some of these 'Frenshams', incidentally, have developed suckers, probably due to their roots being damaged when neighbouring perennials were divided. I slice these out as near to the original root stock as possible.

Like all roses, the 'Frenshams' may need a further trimming of any frost-damaged shoots in late spring, after the final frosts. Once the bushes are in flower there is constant 'summer pruning', or deadheading, to encourage new flowering shoots, as well as for the appearance of each bush. I cut well below the fading flower heads when removing them, and cut tired stems back to a vigorous shooting bud.

Propagating Perennial Lobelia

W E GROW TALL *Lobelia* 'Dark Crusader' in the hot borders, as much for its bronze leaves as for the dark red summer flowers. This half-hardy perennial will survive the winter out of doors in zones where consistently cold weather keeps it dormant, but with us there is the risk that a warm spell will prompt it to put up new shoots which will then be caught by frosts, so we transfer our plants to a cold frame in mid-autumn and divide them in spring.

Having cut down the lobelia stems to about 25cm/10in (*below left*), I dig up the individual plants (*above right*) and put them in a bucket, ready to take behind the scenes to the potting shed. I plant each one up in potting compost, in a 15cm/6in pot, leaving any plantlets that are already coming up attached to the parent (*above, far right*), and firm the soil a little, taking care not to damage the plantlets.

I want my planted-up lobelias to harden

In mid-spring the lobelias begin to send up new shoots, often producing a whole set of new plantlets on the edge of the main crown (*far left*). If you give the pot a sharp knock, compost and plants will slide out on to the potting bench (*left*). Then the little plants can easily be pulled apart (*below left*). Each one is potted up in a separate pot, and the central crown is also repotted. Put a bit of compost in each pot and then, holding the plant with one hand (*bottom left*), press additional compost in around the edge and over the roots until the pot is filled up to about 2.5cm/1in below the rim (it is always a good idea to leave a space between the soil surface and the rim, for ease of watering). Gently firm the compost around the plant (*bottom right*).

The pots should remain in a cold frame, with the lid left off as the weather warms up, for gradual hardening off, until they are put out in their flowering site in late spring.

By this simple process you can easily double the number of your plants – the very nicest part of gardening.

off, so initially I put them in a cold frame with the lid open (*left*). However, the frame must be closed as soon as frost is threatened. The lobelia stems are cut down a bit more before the frame is closed. They will die back during the winter. Remove the stem at the base when it has died, as otherwise it may rot and kill the whole clump.

Perennial Lobelia 155

Small-flowered Clematis

Clematis cirrhosa var. *balearica*

I FIND THE small-flowered species and hybrid clematis infinitely valuable as companion plants. They have a natural appearance better suited to my sort of gardening than the artificial, almost blowzy look of their cousins the large-flowered hybrids. (Although in contradiction to this I have a tender affection for some of the more bizarre doubles, when they are used deliberately to make an exotic statement.)

None of the small-flowered clematis is too flamboyant or attention-seeking, and they associate perfectly with other plants; they clothe high walls or tumble down low ones, mingle with other climbing vines without overrunning them, and scramble through branches of deciduous trees and shrubs. A clematis can be chosen to flower at the same time as the host plant, and intertwine with its blossom – a pink variety of *Clematis montana* weaving through a spring cherry or crab apple. Or it can fit into a scheme of flowery progression – a fruit tree with May blossom, a rambling June rose and a late-flowering clematis can all be grown together.

There are so many different types of clematis that, in a temperate climate, it is possible to have one in flower at almost every season. At Tintinhull we have two winter/early-spring clematis, *C. cirrhosa* var. *balearica* and *C. armandii*, both evergreen. The former, from the Mediterranean, has fern-like leaves and bears its greeny-cream bells during mild spells in the winter, with a final burst in March and April. The later-flowering scented *C. armandii*, from Asia, has handsome almost leathery leaves, translucent when young, and trusses of scented cream flowers. Both these clematis will thrive on a warm wall – in full sun for

C. cirrhosa var. *balearica*, part shade for *C. armandii* – but are also vigorous scramblers if allowed to twine free in the branches of a host tree or large shrub. In Mediterranean climates I have seen these clematis draping tall cypresses with blossom in midwinter.

The real spring season starts with the Alpina clematis, unobtrusive flowerers which seem to blossom indiscriminately in sun or shade. They begin at Tintinhull in

April, but late frosts may damage flower buds. My favourite of the Alpinas is *C.a.* 'Frances Rivis', blue to blueish-purple with long sepals. The *C. macropetala* cultivars are similar but in deeper blue and purple shades.

The montanas come next, thugs compared to other spring clematis, and vigorous enough to clamber into tall trees. The type *C. montana* is white, the named variations are pale to dusky pink and all are fragrant. I prefer the white species or one of the paler pinks such as 'Pink Perfection', although the darker 'Picton's Variety' appeals when draped against grey stone. Another variety, *C.m.* var. *wilsonii*, flowers in June and July with narrow creamy-white flowers, just after its host, *Malus hupehensis*, has carpeted the lawn in fallen blossom outside my bedroom window. Christopher Lloyd describes *C.m.* var. *wilsonii* as giving off 'great wafts of hot chocolate aroma'.

At Hadspen I had beginner's luck with *C. florida* 'Sieboldii', perhaps the most beautiful of all clematis, producing in early summer flowers like a passion flower, white sepals framing clustered petal-like bright purple stamens flecked with pale pink. It is notoriously temperamental: give it star treatment and a sheltered corner.

After this there is a pause before the Texensis and Viticella clematis. The Texans include 'Duchess of Albany', with bell-shaped pink flowers, 'Etoile Rose', with nodding bell-shaped sepals that are silvery pink on the outside and a deep cherry-purple within, and the crimson 'Gravetye Beauty'. All the available Viticella clematis are worth growing. My favourites are 'Alba Luxurians', which has white sepals with green recurved tips, 'Etoile Violette', with purple sepals, double-flowered 'Purpurea Plena Elegans', 'Royal Velours', a dark rich velvety purple, and *C. viticella* itself, with delicate nodding purple flowers. Then there is 'Huldine', a hybrid with some Viticella genes, which starts flowering in midsummer – July here – and continues into autumn. With flowers 10 cm/4in across, 'Huldine' is the largest-flowered clematis I really like. White sepals are mauve-tinged beneath.

Other late-season flowerers include *C. campaniflora*, with blueish-white bell flowers, *C. flammula*, with deliciously fragrant creamy blossom, the lemon-peel *C. tibetana* ssp. *vernayi* (*C. orientalis* of gardens) and *C. tangutica*. In Britain the last clematis to flower is the cowslip-scented *C. rehderiana*, but in many American gardens, where hotter summers provide more suitable conditions, the glorious white *C. terniflora* (sometimes listed as *C. paniculata* or *C. maximowicziana*) produces a spectacular late-autumn display.

Clematis do require careful siting; they like to search for the sun to flower but need their roots in cool shade. A host shrub will often provide sufficient protection from hot sun, but a position on a wall may get too hot and dry unless the roots are shaded (even a flat stone may be sufficient). All clematis enjoy a mulch in spring and this, as well as encouraging growth, will help keep the soil moist and the roots cool.

Although once established these small-flowered clematis are less trouble than the larger-flowered types and seem more robust, they do benefit from regular attention through the summer. Tendrils, the climbing leaf stalks, need guiding to encourage the flowering shoots to spread out into broad fan-like shapes of colour. (The pruner's task is simplified if they are grown on a wall on a structure of wire or trelliswork.) My husband John used to do this twiddly work meticulously, visiting each clematis in the garden at least once a week. I am too impatient to get perfect results.

When it comes to pruning you can follow specific directions for each type, but the main thing to know – as in all pruning – is whether the clematis flowers on old or new wood. Generally speaking, the harder you cut back in winter the later a clematis will flower – so, at pruning time, you can draw out the length of the flowering period by cutting shoots of any one specimen to different lengths.

On pages 158–9, left to right:
Clematis alpina 'Frances Rivis'
Clematis florida 'Sieboldii'
Clematis 'Etoile Violette'

Clematis 'Duchess of Albany'

Clematis flammula

Companionable Salvias

THERE HAS RECENTLY been an explosion in the numbers of different sages available, with flowers covering a huge colour range from scarlet through purple and violet to azure-blue, white and even pale yellow. Many of them make superb garden plants, wonderful for drifts in borders or growing in containers.

Although variable, most salvia flowers have a distinctive upper petal arching forward to resemble the shape of a hood, with calyces and petals often of contrasting hues. Some flowers gape open, others are nearly tubular.

Although all sages need a sunny, well-protected site to give of their best flowering, the common European sage, *Salvia officinalis*, and some of its relatives – such as *S. lavandulifolia* – are hardy to -20°C/-4°F. Most of the more tender sages are easily propagated from seed or cuttings, so can be grown as annuals. The common sage and those from dry areas in California are drought-resistant, but most of the South American sages need plenty of moisture during the summer.

THE BLUE TONES

My favourite salvias are the blues, in all their shades and tints of pure azure, mauve, violet and lavender. At Bettiscombe I plan to have a border of blue salvias, perhaps with some silvery-leaved artemisias and dorycniums added to make the blues seem even brighter.

At Tintinhull I have, at various times, used groups of the sky-blue South American perennial *S. uliginosa* in the pale borders in the Pool Garden, less formally as drifts in the Middle Garden and, most effectively, clumped in pots in the

Salvia uliginosa

Salvia cacaliifolia

Salvia patens 'Cambridge Blue'

summerhouse. Tall and graceful, it needs a sheltered position with plenty of moisture and does not like competition from neighbouring plants. A tender perennial salvia, the compact dark blue *S. cacaliifolia* from Mexico, is one of the most floriferous of the sages, flowering even in semi-shade and doing especially well in containers. We take cuttings every year. *S. leptophylla* (*S. reptans*), also from Mexico, is smaller in its flowering parts but makes a suckering bushy plant in a pot. I leave it, in its pot, in a greenhouse to die down in winter and reshoot in spring. *S. leucantha*, the tender Mexican sage bush, with chenille-textured violet to lavender flower spikes, thrives without much watering and is especially suitable for pots. It is a late-summer performer in Britain but in its native habitat and in California it flowers all winter. We take cuttings each autumn and overwinter them free of frost.

We grow the bright blue Mexican *S. patens*, the paler 'Cambridge Blue' and

Right: *Salvia leucantha*

The Pea Family

WE ALL DEVELOP preferences for certain plants, finding that, over and over again, and in a variety of situations, they fulfil our expectations. Many years ago I found that goat's rue, *Galega officinalis*, and its cousin *G. orientalis* were important in any border I made. *G. officinalis* and its many modern colour types, with pea flowers varying between pale lavender-blue, lilac, pink and white, produce their massed blooms in midsummer. The vivid darker blue flowers of *G. orientalis* are earlier.

Galegas are Leguminosae, members of the extensive pea family, which includes trees, shrubs, climbers, perennials and annuals. Among the perennials, another essential border plant is the drought-resistant lupin-like false indigo, *Baptisia australis*, a North American native with long racemes of blue flowers carried on erect branching stems clothed with blue-green foliage. It is beautiful all summer, as imposing as a shrub, and by autumn carries decorative black seed pods. The smaller *B. leucantha* has white flowers slightly tinged with purple.

We have no space for the true garden lupins at Tintinhull but have, instead, grown specimens of the tender blue-flowered shrubby *Lupinus albifrons* var. *douglasii* from California. Its silvery-silk leaves and violet flowers make it a superlative pot plant. We also grow the yellow tree lupin, *L. arboreus*.

Indigoferas and lespedezas are also members of the pea family. Both are shrubs to 1m/3ft or so but respond best in the garden to being cut down to the ground

Baptisia australis

mauve 'Chilcombe' as annuals from both seed and cuttings. They will usually appear again if left in a flower bed but do better if propagated each season. *S. discolor* from Peru has flowers of such a dark violet-blue they appear almost black. We grow it in containers, but I have seen it growing more luxuriously in open ground. It is not at all winter-hardy, so we take cuttings each year.

The common sage, *S. officinalis*, an evergreen shrub from the Mediterranean area, makes a low-growing bush (to 75cm/30in), as useful for foliage as for flowers. *S.o.* 'Icterina' has variegated golden leaves, 'Purpurascens' has reddish-purple foliage and 'Tricolor' has leaves three-toned grey-green, with pink to red marks.

Both the annual clary, *S. viridis*, and biennial *S. sclarea* var. *turkestanica* have flower bracts that are a mixture of white, pink and blue. In *S.s.* var. *turkestanica* the stems are pink-tinted too.

THE REDS

Except in climates where they can be grown outside all through the year (as I find is possible in California and in Texas), I prefer to grow most of the shrubby red-flowered salvias in pots. *S. elegans* and *S. microphylla* varieties are all easy to overwinter if you have a greenhouse. If left outside some of the microphyllas will behave like sub-shrubs and shoot again from the base in spring. At Tintinhull both *S. elegans* and *S. fulgens* make splashes of scarlet in the hot borders.

There are many more salvias to experiment with – it would be a lifetime's work to learn their names and how to use them well in the garden.

Salvia discolor

Salvia elegans

Galega officinalis

Lathyrus vernus

Lupinus arboreus

each spring. They need full sun and adequate drainage. *Indigofera heterantha* from the Himalaya has rosy-lilac flowers carried for two months in late summer. Pink *I. kirilowii*, indigo bush, grown successfully in the southern states of America, is also worth attempting in sheltered gardens in cooler climates. The pink and white forms of bush clover, *Lespedeza thunbergii*, are very similar: branching silky sprays are covered in crimson-purple pea flowers in the last months of the season.

Sweet peas are invaluable in the garden. Most often grown as climbers, some will also make sprawling bushes or weave between other plants. Everyone knows and loves *Lathyrus odoratus*, the annual sweet pea, which comes in every colour from white through pink, lavender, crimson and violet-blue to almost black. Grown up tripods in the Kitchen Garden, they make scented columns of colour. The late-flowering perennial pea, *L. latifolius*, will trail down a bank, smother a hedge with blossom, and, in a border scheme, disguise

the dying leaves and flowers of earlier-flowering perennials. We have it in one of the borders at Tintinhull but at Bettiscombe I will grow it to rampage over my olive trees. The Persian everlasting pea, *L. rotundifolius*, with salmon-pink flowers, is earlier; at Tintinhull it grows up each year into an early rose, 'Shot Silk'. Lord Anson's blue pea, *L. nervosus*, is tender but worth growing at the base of a warm wall. It has fragrant pale blue flowers and silver leaves. *L. vernus*, with dark purple or pale pink flowers, makes a low bush hardly more than 30cm/1ft high. Very hardy and thriving in well-drained but poor soil, it has ferny, much-divided leaves, which, when interspersed with the small flowers, make an attractive spring mound. It almost vanishes through the summer months but gradually increases its spread as well as seeding in neighbouring corners. I planted it at Tintinhull to give spring effects at the back of the Pool Garden pale borders, and have it at Bettiscombe among golden foliage and lime-green flowerers.

Surrounded by trees – magnolias and old yew trees to the south, the dominant cedar on the northern edge – walls and yew hedging, the Cedar Court, with its central lawn, provides an oasis, a moment of calm after the busy, colourful planting in many other areas of the garden.

THE CEDAR COURT

IN MANY GARDENS, especially in towns, it is the central lawn, a well of green, which provides the setting with a focal point, as pleasing as reflecting water. Most often the lawn is shaped geometrically as a square, rectangle, circle or oval, with some strategically placed trees to silhouette the sky and balance with the mass of the house. Surrounding borders of shrubs and flowers hide perimeter fences or walls to complete the garden design. It is the simplest and often the most satisfying garden arrangement. A green oasis, the lawn also provides a natural recreation area for children and dogs, bridging that awkward gap between the gardener's love of planting and the family's need for an open space.

The lawn in the Cedar Court at Tintinhull fits into this pattern. Its simple greenness, almost uninterrupted by planting, comes as a relief after the more elaborate schemes elsewhere in the garden.

Its layout of a central lawn surrounded by broad borders follows the form of a multitude of other gardens. Although several beds have been carved out for spring-flowering magnolias, the grass, mown in traditional stripes with a cylinder mower, almost forms a square. On the south side it is edged with a broad stone-flagged pavement, in which grow two ancient yew trees; on the north it stretches up to a cedar of Lebanon, probably planted at the beginning of the nineteenth century. Although it has lost many of its spreading lower branches and now has a very sparse outline, this cedar still dominates the garden. Sadly, it has become dangerous, the main

Although much smaller than the lawn of the Cedar Court, the lawn in this Michigan garden is just as much of a haven.

trunk being rotten at its core, and is to be removed. Under the cedar, golden aconites and narcissi and mauve *Crocus tommasinianus* flower early in the year but, as the leaves fade by April, mowing is not interrupted. A wide west-facing border is backed by a high stone wall on which roses, clematis and honeysuckle have a chance to run riot. Sheltered by a yew hedge, Phyllis Reiss's foliage scheme of golden and purple, enhanced by flowers in rich crimson and blue, lies in part shade on the western fringe. The lawn itself is large enough to allow children's games.

The care of grass is certainly not labour-saving; almost any other planting of parterre beds surrounded by hard pathways would be less demanding of time and attention. After being scarified to remove mossy thatch during the winter or early spring, the grass in the Cedar Court is fertilized and treated with a selective herbicide as the growing season begins. It is cut and edged twenty-nine times in an average year, the last mowing often being in a mild spell in December (it is important not to walk on it when it is frost-covered). The areas under the yews and under the cedar need watering in dry periods. In spite of all this work I cannot imagine not having one lawn area in a garden. Usually when I am advising on a garden anywhere in Britain, especially if it is in a small urban space, I will recommend a traditional central lawn (provided always there is enough sun).

Small-flowered narcissi flourish among the leaves of winter aconites and crocus under the old cedar. The grass is cut six weeks after the daffodils have finished flowering.

In my walled garden at Bettiscombe, a lawn, decorated with yew pyramids, is the main garden feature revealed from the house windows. This grass is almost completely surrounded by a yew hedge which, eventually, will effectively screen detailed planting schemes in the rest of this sheltered area from immediate view. I love the idea of secret hidden surprises to be discovered in progression and I find that the smaller the whole garden area the more important it is to erect vertical screens and create separate sections; this increases the feeling of overall space. On the approach side at the front of the house, where the landscape is open, more yew pyramids, this time reinforced by an outer avenue of mulberries, march down the centre of the field to frame an oak tree. The mown grass which sets off the yews merges to make a neat edge with rougher grass, cut monthly during the summer, at the sides – grass which ultimately will become a meadow for naturalized bulbs and flowers, an advantage over Tintinhull where there was no space for this. Hornbeam hedges outline formal French-style alleys of cut grass, as well as hiding future utility and vegetable areas.

The Bettiscombe garden has many of the features of Tintinhull but promises to need much less skilled maintenance. Although grass-cutting and hedge-trimming are labour-intensive, the labour need not be highly trained: both activities require good machines rather than specialized knowledge. In future years the lawns, in both the walled garden and the outer area, and the yew pyramids (by then I hope 4.5m/15ft tall) and yew and hornbeam hedges (probably to 3m/10ft) may well be the only features which are properly maintained, and any flower bed untidiness in surrounding areas will be hidden from immediate view.

At Tintinhull the Cedar Court could be a much simpler scheme than it is. The borders, which do demand attention, could be dispensed with, leaving the trees, including the dominant cedar, the dark colonnade of yews, the grass and the five magnolias – *Magnolia grandiflora* against a south-facing wall, *M. × soulangeana* nearby in a circular bed carpeted with ivy-leaved cyclamen, *M. stellata* and two large specimens of *M. liliiflora* 'Nigra' in square beds on the south side, underplanted with hellebores and Welsh poppies. All this provides sufficient interest without additional frills; and for a weekend gardener it would be quite enough work. In fact, of course, at Tintinhull we make few concessions to reducing maintenance, and managing the existing Cedar Court borders has given me a great deal of pleasure.

In spring, before its leaves unfurl, the wide-spreading Magnolia liliiflora *'Nigra' bears erect goblet-shaped flowers, deep purple on the outside and stained with cream within. Nearby, under the cedar, the hybrid* M. × soulangeana *is also in flower.*

The Purple and Gold Border

The flowers of Sambucus nigra *'Guincho Purple', borne in broad heads on purple stalks, are pink in bud and open to pink on the outside and white within. Its bronze leaf tones work beautifully with the other foliage colours in the border, linking the darker purples and the brighter golds.*

PROBABLY THE GOLD AND purple foliage bed is the best known of all Mrs Reiss's schemes. Gold-variegated dogwoods (*Cornus alba* 'Spaethii'), with startling crimson stems in winter – we cut these back almost to the ground in spring every other year – alternate with purple, copper and bronze foliage plants. Surprisingly, she did not plant the purple-leaved smoke bush she used so frequently throughout the rest of the garden, but she included *Berberis thunbergii* 'Atropurpurea Nana' and *B.* × *ottawensis* 'Superba', the latter one of the best barberries, with yellow and red berries.

Various plants have been added over the years. I have to admit that we were quite pleased when a large *Prunus* × *blireana* keeled over in a storm in 1989. This gave us room to plant two more berberis, *Berberis dictophylla* var. *approximata* (which unfortunately died in 1990) and *B. temolaica*. These are rarer because they are hard to propagate, but they are perhaps the most attractive of all berberis, with distinctive glaucous foliage and young stems covered with a soft bloom. Other additions have been the dark-leaved elder *Sambucus nigra* 'Guincho Purple', and spring-flowering *Viburnum sargentii* 'Onondaga', with bronze young foliage, both toning down the strongest gold/purple contrasts.

All the flowers in this border contain some blue pigment which harmonizes with the dusky foliage. Crimson and pink shrub roses – rose 'Fellenberg', 'Rosemary Rose' with purple-flushed leaves, the Hybrid Musk 'Cornelia', thornless 'Zéphirine Drouhin' and *Rosa glauca*, with its blue-grey leaves and pink flowers – all presenting their best performance in June but also, if deadheaded, providing an almost continual display through the rest of the summer. In spring the bed is carpeted with blue scillas and drifts of *Anemone apennina*, with a corner clump of Solomon's seal, the ordinary *Polygonatum* × *hybridum*. The shrubs are interplanted with vigorous perennials and some annuals, all with dusky purple or bright blue flowers. For blue effects in early summer *Veronica austriaca* ssp. *teucrium* tumbles over the stone edging, while blue salvias – *Salvia patens*, most satisfactory

In the purple and gold border the young shoots of Cornus alba *'Spaethii' contrast with the duller purples of berberis and the bronze foliage of bright-flowered 'Rosemary Rose'. Towards the back of the border is thornless 'Zéphirine Drouhin' with paler pink flowers. Geranium nodosum flowers along the edge, with* Veronica austriaca *ssp.* teucrium *and silver-leaved* Salvia argentea.

if grown each year from seed, and *S. guaranitica*, which is hardy if adequately mulched – flower later and continue into the first frosts. Dark velvet-flowered *Clematis* 'Jackmanii' grows on umbrella-shaped frames. Eupatoriums and bronze-leaved sedums, lythrums and prized *Vernonia* species, brought back as seed from the United States, are late performers and will seed quite prolifically if given the opportunity.

Personally, I so much enjoy the sultry blue-toned colours that if I were redesigning this border today I would probably omit the golden-leaved elements and use green-leaved forms of red-stemmed dogwood for the decorative winter effect. But I remember my inspiring first visit to Tintinhull thirty-five years ago and the impression this foliage border made on my totally untutored eyes. The colour combinations seemed to be just perfect. Over the years I believe Mrs Reiss's scheme has influenced a number of other new gardeners, convincing them that the colour, shape and texture of leaves are at least as important as ephemeral flower colours. In my old garden at Hadspen, in the central border of the kitchen garden, Nori and Sandra Pope now use a mixture of plants with golden, grey and glaucous leaves – euphorbias in quantity, alchemillas and grasses, enlivened by washes of blue-flowered perennials, but with flowers of minimal importance.

Rosa 'Fellenberg'

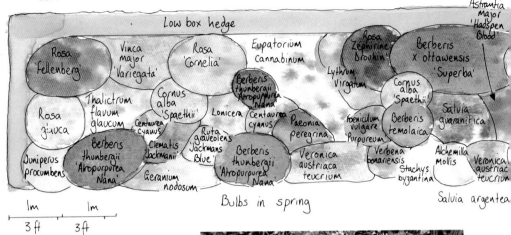

Low box hedge

Rosa 'Fellenberg'

Vinca major 'Variegata'

Rosa 'Cornelia'

Eupatorium cannabinum

Rosa 'Zéphirine Drouhin'

Berberis x ottawensis 'Superba'

Astrantia major 'Hadspen Blood'

Lythrum virgatum

Thalictrum flavum glaucum

Cornus alba 'Spaethii'

Berberis thunbergii 'Atropurpurea Nana'

Cornus alba 'Spaethii'

Rosa glauca

Lonicera

Centaurea cyanus

Foeniculum vulgare 'Purpureum'

Berberis temolaica

Salvia guaranitica

Juniperus procumbens

Berberis thunbergii 'Atropurpurea Nana'

Centaurea cyanus

Ruta graveolens 'Jackmans Blue'

Clematis 'Jackmanii'

Paeonia peregrina

Berberis thunbergii 'Atropurpured Nana'

Verbena bonariensis

Alchemilla mollis

Veronica austriac teucrium

Geranium nodosum

Veronica austriaca teucrium

Stachys byzantina

Salvia argentea

Bulbs in spring

1m 1m
3ft 3ft

Lonicera periclymenum 'Serotina'

Geranium nodosum

Rosa 'Zéphirine Drouhin'

Astrantia major 'Hadspen Blood'

Foeniculum vulgare 'Purpureum'

Veronica austriaca ssp. *teucrium*

174 THE CEDAR COURT

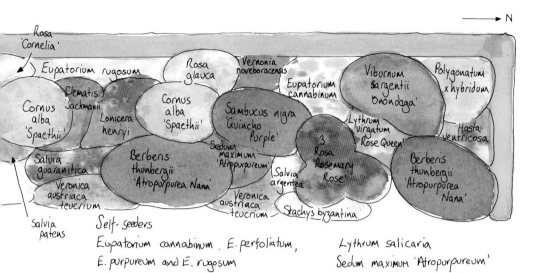

Rosa
'Cornelia'

Eupatorium rugosum

Clematis 'Jackmanii'

Rosa glauca

Vernonia noveboracensis

Eupatorium cannabinum

Viburnum sargentii 'Onondaga'

Polygonatum x hybridum

Cornus alba 'Spaethii'

Lonicera henryi

Cornus alba 'Spaethii'

Sambucus nigra 'Guincho Purple'

Lythrum virgatum 'Rose Queen'

Hosta ventricosa

Salvia guaranitica

Berberis thunbergii 'Atropurpurea Nana'

Sedum maximum 'Atropurpureum'

3 Rosa 'Rosemary Rose'

Berberis thunbergii 'Atropurpurea Nana'

Veronica austriaca teucrium

Salvia argentea

Veronica austriaca teucrium

Stachys byzantina

Salvia patens

N

Self-seeders

Eupatorium cannabinum, E. perfoliatum,
E. purpureum and E. rugosum

Lythrum salicaria
Sedum maximum 'Atropurpureum'
Vernonia noveboracensis

Lythrum virgatum 'Rose Queen'

Rosa 'Cornelia'

Cornus alba 'Spaethii'

Rosa 'Rosemary Rose'

Salvia guaranitica

Stachys byzantina

Salvia argentea

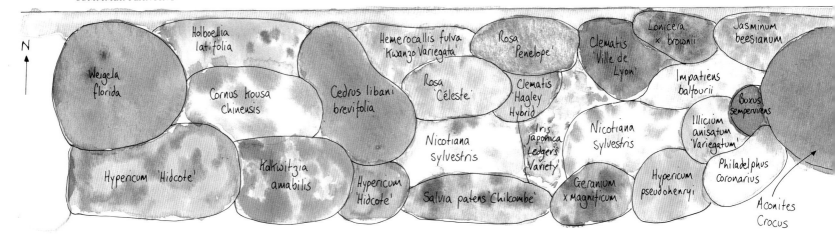

THE CEDAR TREE BORDER

THE CEDAR TREE border is very mixed. Until recently two tree peonies were important here. Sadly, they succumbed to honey fungus, leaving large gaps which we have filled with temporary plantings of *Nicotiana sylvestris*. On the wall behind, the tender Chinese evergreen *Holboellia latifolia* (*H. coriacea* is hardier and very similar), with intensely fragrant white bell-shaped flowers in spring, grows near *Clematis* 'Ville de Lyon', *Lonicera* × *brownii*, *Jasminum beesianum* and the scarlet-flowered California currant, *Ribes speciosum*, which is trained back as a wall shrub to give it maximum protection and heat. *Hedera helix* 'Sagittifolia', with elegant arrow-shaped leaves, clothes the wall above the door, next to my favourite climbing rose, 'Gloire de Dijon'. The invasive – but annually from seed and easily removed – balsam, *Impatiens balfourii*, is allowed to flower in any empty spaces.

Rosa 'Penelope'

Philadelphus coronarius

Kolkwitzia amabilis

Rosa 'Céleste'

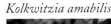

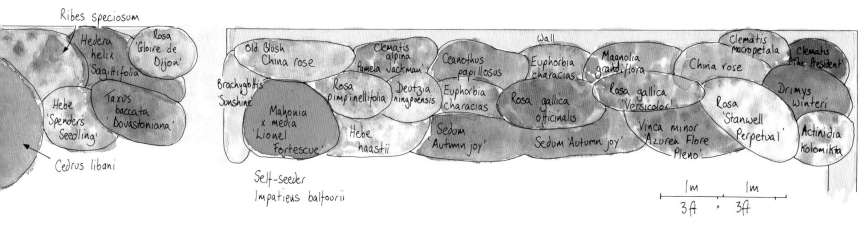

Ribes speciosum

Hedera helix Sagittifolia

Rosa 'Gloire de Dijon'

Hebe 'Spenders Seedling'

Taxus baccata 'Dovastoniana'

Cedrus libani

Old Blush China rose

Clematis alpina 'Pamela Jackman'

Ceanothus papillosus

Wall

Euphorbia characias

Magnolia grandiflora

China rose

Clematis macropetala

Clematis 'The President'

Brachyglottis 'Sunshine'

Mahonia × media 'Lionel Fortescue'

Rosa pimpinellifolia

Deutzia ningpoensis

Euphorbia characias

Rosa gallica officinalis

Rosa gallica 'Versicolor'

Drimys winteri

Hebe haastii

Sedum 'Autumn joy'

Sedum 'Autumn joy'

Vinca minor 'Azurea Flore Pleno'

Rosa 'Stanwell Perpetual'

Actinidia kolomikta

Self-seeder Impatiens balfourii

1m 1m
3ft · 3ft

Ribes speciosum

Old Blush China rose

Rosa gallica 'Versicolor'

Mahonia × media 'Lionel Fortescue'

Drimys winteri

Sedum 'Autumn Joy'

Actinidia kolomikta

The East Border

T HE OTHER MAIN border in the Cedar Court faces west and is deliberately less colour-orientated, with roses, honeysuckle and clematis draping the high wall behind it. It is given overall coherence by fine shrubs such as the tender semi-evergreen *Hoheria* 'Glory of Amlwch' and the darker-leaved Mediterranean *Phillyrea latifolia*, the latter an ideal formal bush or tree for the border. These are interplanted with Hybrid Musk roses such as 'Penelope' and 'Felicia', shrubs like *Escallonia* 'Iveyi', with erect white flower trusses, *Philadelphus* 'Innocence', with white variegated leaves and scented flowers in midsummer, and *Hydrangea aspera* Villosa Group, a glorious sight towards the end of the summer. The bed is edged with alternating groups of catmint and sedum (*Sedum* 'Autumn Joy'), the latter's fleshy glaucous leaves a strong element of the design from spring onwards and beloved by butterflies when in flower in August and September. White epilobiums (*Epilobium angustifolium album*), tall macleayas, white Japanese anemones (*Anemone* × *hybrida* 'Honorine Jobert') and *Aster lateriflorus* 'Horizontalis' spread as drifts in their seasons. *Cornus kousa* var. *chinensis*, with creamy bracts and strawberry-like fruits, backed by an old boxwood tree, is a feature close to the south end of the border.

Separated from this border by a path there is a narrow bed planted with yellow, bronze and dark purple irises. Alliums and annual love-in-a-mist (*Nigella damascena* 'Miss Jekyll') also thrive here. A ribbon of mossy saxifrage (*Saxifraga exarata* ssp. *moschata*) makes a cloud of pink in early summer on the outer edge; pink-flowered colchicums (*Colchicum speciosum*) contribute a similar pattern of colour in early autumn on the inner path side. At the southern end of the iris bed, where it is overhung by the *Magnolia liliiflora*, I have planted some shade-tolerant small plants: shooting stars (*Dodecatheon meadia*), *Geranium phaeum* and wake robins, forms of trillium from the Connecticut woods. In late summer *Hosta* 'Royal Standard' has scented lily-like white flowers rising above apple-green foliage.

Under an Asiatic dogwood, Cornus kousa var. chinensis, *the cottagey mixed planting includes* Symphytum × uplandicum *'Variegatum',* euphorbias, Welsh poppies and the elegant fern-like Selinum tenuifolium. *In the iris bed love-in-a-mist and* Allium christophii *extend the flowering season, while groups of catmint along the front of the wall border unify the colour scheme.*

Escallonia 'Iveyi'

Rosa 'New Dawn'

Clematis 'Pagoda'

Hydrangea macrophylla

SUMMMER PLANTING

'Lavatera Barnsley'

Drimys winteri

Actinidia Kolomikta

Actinidia Kolomikta

Clematis terniflora

Rosa 'New Dawn'

Clematis 'Jackmanii'

Lonicera

Anemone 'Honorine Jobert'

Rosa 'Stanwell Perpetual'

Hydrangea Macrophylla

Escallonia 'Iveyi'

Anemone 'Honorine Jobert'

Macleaya cordata

Hoheria 'Glory of Amlwch'

China rose

Vinca minor 'Azurea Flore Pleno'

Epilobium angustifolium album

Aster lateriflorus 'Horizontalis'

Rosa 'Felicia'

Hydrangea aspera Villosa

Rosa 'Penelope'

Stachys macrantha 'Superba'

Paeonia lactiflora hybrid

Sedum 'Autumn Joy'

Anemone 'Honorine Jobert'

Nepeta 'Six Hills Giant'

Sedum 'Autumn Joy'

1m 1m
3ft 3ft

Self-seeders
Euphorbia stricta
Helleborus foetidus and H xsternii 'Boughton Beauty'
Lunaria annua
Meconopsis cambrica
Nigella damascena 'Miss Jekyll'
Verbena bonariensis

Iris 'Perry Hill', Iris 'Gay Trip' and Iris 'Bronze Bird' with nigella,
Saxifraga exarata moschata

Rosa 'Felicia'

Nigella damascena 'Miss Jekyll'

Hoheria 'Glory of Amlwch'

Clematis heracleifolia var. *davidiana* 'Wyevale'

Lavatera 'Barnsley'

- Vitis davidii
- Begonia grandis evansiana
- Aucuba japonica
- Buxus (tree)
- Cornus alternifolia 'Argentea'
- Sarcococca confusa

N ←

Trachelospermum jasminoides

Symphytum × uplandicum 'Variegatum'

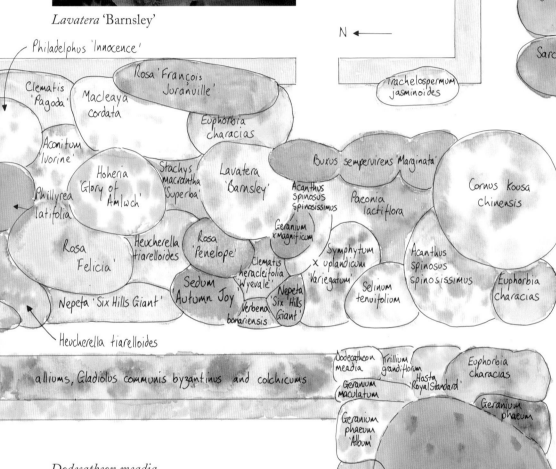

- Philadelphus 'Innocence'
- Clematis 'Pagoda'
- Macleaya cordata
- Rosa 'François Juranville'
- Euphorbia characias
- Aconitum 'Ivorine'
- Hoheria 'Glory of Amlwch'
- Stachys macrantha 'Superba'
- Lavatera 'Barnsley'
- Acanthus spinosus spinosissimus
- Buxus sempervirens 'Marginata'
- Paeonia lactiflora
- Cornus kousa chinensis
- Phillyrea latifolia
- Rosa 'Felicia'
- Heucherella tiarelloides
- Rosa 'Penelope'
- Geranium × magnificum
- Clematis heracleifolia 'Wyevale'
- Symphytum × uplandicum 'Variegatum'
- Acanthus spinosus spinosissimus
- Euphorbia characias
- Sedum Autumn Joy
- Nepeta 'Six Hills Giant'
- Verbena bonariensis
- Nepeta 'Six Hills Giant'
- Selinum tenuifolium
- Nepeta 'Six Hills Giant'
- Heucherella tiarelloides

- alliums, Gladiolus communis byzantinus and colchicums
- Dodecatheon meadia
- Trillium grandiflorum
- Euphorbia characias
- Geranium maculatum
- Hosta 'Royal Standard'
- Geranium phaeum 'Album'
- Geranium phaeum
- Helleborus × sternii 'Boughton Beauty'
- Magnolia liliiflora 'Nigra'
- Meconopsis cambrica
- Hemerocallis fulva 'Kwanzo Variegata'

Selinum tenuifolium

Dodecatheon meadia

Trillium grandiflorum

The Magnolia Beds

On the north side of the Cedar Court, *Magnolia × soulangeana* has autumn-flowering ivy-leaved *Cyclamen hederifolium* growing in a large circle around its trunk; during the winter the marbled leaves set off the silver-grey bark and purple-tinged twigs. In the south-west corner the low spreading branches of another *M. liliiflora* 'Nigra', with *M. stellata* at its side, create a woodland situation for spring bulbs and shade-tolerant herbaceous plants such as daylilies, erythroniums, crane's-bill geraniums and hellebores – a mixture of *Helleborus foetidus* and the hybrid *H. × sternii* 'Boughton Beauty', both of which seed prolifically. Clumps of Welsh poppies make a yellow wash in season in these shady beds, but their ready seeding habit is less desirable, as they tend to appear throughout the garden and an established seedling is difficult to eradicate in routine weeding. They should be deadheaded as soon as they finish flowering: they can easily become weeds where not wanted and, small though they are, the glimmering yellow flowers catch the eye to spoil a planned colour scheme. This poppy and the Byzantine gladiolus, both desirable plants in their place, had escaped into many beds when we came in 1979; it took several seasons of weeding to contain them. Under one of the magnolias we also have the almost evergreen crane's-bill *Geranium nodosum*, with lilac flowers and glossy leaves, which drifts out under the spreading magnolia and seeds into the adjacent border.

The ivy-leaved Cyclamen hederifolium *from the Mediterranean region which carpets the round bed under* Magnolia × soulangeana *flowers for six weeks in late August and September and most years will survive the occasional sharp frost. Its leaves are attractive all winter, fading only in May, after which the bed is mulched.*

Mushroom compost can be stockpiled and will improve if left to rot down over a few years. We find it useful throughout the garden at Tintinhull but especially under the magnolias, which we mulch heavily, covering the ground to a depth of 10 cm/4 in. In the neutral soil they might easily develop chlorosis, but the humus-making mulch keeps them healthy. The cyclamen benefit too, and now make a dense mat.

THE SOUTH SIDE

A WIDE FLOWER BED under the shady north wall of the house grows a collection of hybrids and varieties of *Rosa pimpinellifolia*, all of which flower well before the first June flush of roses in the rest of the garden. Mixed in between the roses are Solomon's seal, white-flowered foxgloves and the hardy twining flame flower, *Tropaeolum speciosum*, with scarlet flowers in late summer. This perennial nasturtium, often seen in northern gardens growing over tall dark yew hedges, is difficult to establish but seems to thrive at Tintinhull. It must have been there for many years. The climbing shade-tolerant rose 'Madame Grégoire Staechelin' has double pink flowers in early June. A spreading *Cotoneaster horizontalis* frames and softens the wide steps to the outer courtyard. In spring tulips grow in the reconstituted stone pots and orange- and red-flowered mimulus, grown each year from cuttings, are used for summer decoration.

To the west, sheltered by the two old yews, another border provides more opportunity for shade-lovers. It has Oregon grape (*Mahonia aquifolium*), viburnums and winter-flowering scented evergreen *Ribes laurifolium*. Scotch burnet roses are interplanted with the maple-leaved perennial *Kirengeshoma palmata*, with primrose shuttlecock flowers in late summer, and a glossy-leaved toad lily, *Tricyrtis formosana*, undercarpeted with groups of *Lamium* 'White Nancy' and Miss Jekyll's favourite fumitory, *Corydalis cheilanthifolia*, with fern-like leaves and pale flowers. Against the wall and almost clothing part of it, the vigorous climber *Sinofranchetia chinensis* thrives but finds it too shady to flower.

Right: *The little ferny corydalis,* Corydalis cheilanthifolia, *one of Miss Jekyll's favourites, grows in dry shade, along with self-seeded cyclamen and chionodoxa, under one of the yew trees in the Cedar Court.*

Left: *The varieties and hybrids of* Rosa pimpinellifolia *will grow, and be spread by suckers, even in deep shade. At Tintinhull* Rosa × harisonii *'Harison's Yellow' and various Scotch burnet roses thrive under the north wall of the house. The climbing Hybrid Tea rose 'Madame Grégoire Staechelin' flowers on the same wall.*

In the Cedar Court reconstituted stone pots are packed with white lamium and orange- and red-flowered mimulus, plants which prefer the light shade on the north side of the house.

Planting out Annuals

ANNUALS GROWN FROM seed sown in early spring, together with tender woody plants rooted from cuttings during the previous autumn, are indispensable at Tintinhull, carrying colour schemes right through the first frosts and infilling so that no bare earth is left visible or allowed to dry out. Many of the annuals go where spring bulbs such as tulips have finished flowering and have been lifted. Others augment a newly planted border scheme for one or two seasons until shrubs and perennials grow together. Perennials can be divided in autumn or spring and replanted to allow space for clumps of annuals. Occasionally a large shrub dies unexpectedly and the gap provides a perfect site for taller, larger-leaved annuals or biennials.

In the Cedar Court two of our treasured tree peonies in the border under the cedar began to fade out at the end of one season. We left them in position until the following spring, hoping for a recovery, but when we finally realized that the ground was probably

infected with honey fungus, we resigned ourselves to taking them out. Fortunately we had available some trays of tobacco plants, *Nicotiana sylvestris*, a relatively shade-tolerant annual.

We had sown the nicotiana seed in February, pricked the seedlings out into deep trays in March, and gradually hardened the plants off in closed and then open frames in preparation for planting out, which should ideally have been at the end of May.

Because we were late in planting (it was early June before we took out the tree peonies), it was especially important to water the ground thoroughly (*opposite,*

below) before putting in the well-rooted plants. The trays were also soaked in a tank of water until all air-bubbles disappeared. As in all the well-worked Tintinhull borders, the soil is friable and, once it was moistened, it was easy to a dig a hole for each plant (*opposite, above*). I added a handful of dried organic manure before putting the plant in and firming the earth around it (*left, top to bottom*). Positioning the plants 20–30cm/8–12in apart, there was room for a fairly large group in the gap left by one of the tree peonies. Finally, a mulch was applied around the plants to help retain moisture during the months ahead. They flowered in the autumn (*below*).

The Stately Magnolias

THE SOUTHERN OR EVERGREEN magnolia, *Magnolia grandiflora*, from the south-eastern states of North America, is pre-eminent. In California and Mediterranean countries, as well as in the southern states, this wonderful magnolia is to be seen growing in the open, making a shapely pyramid and flowering prolifically. In a temperate climate it needs the protection of a warm wall; even there it may not produce its lemon-scented cream globes until it is at least fifteen years old, and then only spasmodically. None the less, *M. grandiflora* is handsome enough in year-round leaf and habit to merit a prominent garden place. An old specimen, growing espalier-like to the eaves of a house, is a treasure beyond price.

To get flowers on young plants, choose one of the recommended hybrids or cultivars. *M.* 'Maryland' flowered for Graham Stuart Thomas in its second year. I have used *M.g.* 'Goliath', with polished soft elliptic leaves, reddish-brown felted below. *M.g.* 'Exmouth' is similar, and both flower early in life. At Bettiscombe I grow the American *M.g.* 'Little Gem', which is less vigorous and more suitable for a limited space. Probably the hardiest of all these southern magnolias is the excellent hybrid *M.g.* 'Edith Bogue'.

Another evergreen magnolia is *M. delavayi*, with huge sea-green glaucous leaves and creamy-white scented flowers, but this is definitely tender and, without protection, only for favoured localities.

These are the only genuine evergreens among the cultivated magnolias, but there are many deciduous magnolias which are good for integrating into a shrub scheme, with small plants growing under their branches. Tree-like or bushy, all have fragrant blossoms. Some have upright tulip-shaped flowers (*M.* × *soulangeana* and *M. liliiflora*), others have saucer-shaped open flowers (*M. sieboldii* ssp. *sinensis*), and others, such as *M. kobus* and *M. stellata*, have many-petalled small flowers.

We would all love to succeed with some of the earliest flowerers such as the giant Himalayan pink tulip tree, *M. campbellii*, and *M.c.* ssp. *mollicomata*, which flower gloriously in early spring, their pink blossoms outlined against blue skies, in some Cornish gardens and in California.

However, in less favoured areas the buds are almost inevitably damaged by frosts. The flower buds of *M.c.* 'Charles Raffill' are reputedly more resistant. The goblet-shaped buds open like water lilies to display paler pink inside the petals.

Among the more weather-resistant tulip- or goblet-shaped flowerers you can hardly beat the old favourite *M.* × *soulangeana* and its variants, with flowers in different pinks or white. At Tintinhull the type plant stands as a feature in the Cedar Court, where it flowers, leafless, in April. In the

Magnolia grandiflora

Magnolia × *soulangeana* 'Lennei'

Magnolia liliiflora 'Nigra'

same lawn are two large spreading *M. liliiflora* 'Nigra' and a Japanese star magnolia, *M. stellata*. Shrubby in habit and seldom exceeding 3m/10ft in height and spread, *M. stellata* has frost-resistant grey hairy buds during winter and also flowers early while leafless. The flowers of the type are snow-white tinged with pink but there are many darker pink cultivars. The hybrids of *M.* × *loebneri* have much charm. With the habit of *M. stellata* but growing larger, *M.* × *l.* 'Leonard Messel' has petals with the outer surface of lavender-purple, the inner distinctly paler.

One way around the problem of late frosts is to grow only the summer flowerers, such as my favourite deciduous magnolia, *M. virginiana*, the American sweet bay. The leaves, in warm climates almost evergreen, are long and glossy above, glaucous beneath, and it has small cream globular flowers from mid- to late summer. *M. sieboldii*, *M.s.* ssp. *sinensis* and *M. wilsonii* have pendent saucer-shaped flowers in midsummer. *M.* × *wiesneri* (*M. watsonii*), needing acid soil, bears its upward-facing saucer-shaped fragrant flowers a bit later.

The list is endless; we would all love to be magnolia collectors but most of us are severely limited by space. Give those you grow the best possible conditions, with shelter from cold winds and plenty of moisture at the roots during the growing period. When planting prepare a wide hole, at least double the width of the container or root system, add a generous supply of organic matter and plant so that the main root system is only just below the soil surface. All ideally prefer acid soil, but except for those few (such as *M. salicifolia* and *M.* × *wiesneri*) which are definitely calcifuge, most will tolerate some alkalinity, provided they are given plenty of lime-free organic matter to satisfy the shallow, questing roots. Magnolias seldom need pruning. Any shaping necessary should be done after flowering for the deciduous magnolias, in spring for the evergreens.

Magnolia × *loebneri* 'Leonard Messel'

Magnolia stellata

Magnolia wilsonii

Gardening with Cyclamen

THE GARDENING season opens for me each year with the enjoyment of my favourite of all small woodland cyclamens, the spring-flowering *Cyclamen repandum*. The flower smells of violets and is distinctive, with carmine-red – or sometimes pink, or white – upswept, slightly twisted flower petals held above pointed, silver-patterned leaves. This cyclamen needs shade – its leaves will burn in full sun – thriving at Tintinhull under the evergreen oaks as it would in the Mediterranean basin from which it originates. It seeds itself happily and prolifically between ivy and periwinkles, under hellebores and in cracks of paving, and will thrive where water is scarce through most of the year.

In fact *C. repandum* likes exactly the same situation in a garden as the hardier, more vigorous, late-summer-flowering *C. hederifolium*, the most easily grown of all the outdoor cyclamen. *C. hederifolium*, widely distributed all round the Mediterranean, has large scented carmine or white flowers with sharply pointed petals. At Tintinhull the first flowers come in early August and increase in spread and vigour, lasting a good six weeks. The leaves come after the flowers, but start to emerge before the flowering period is over. They are attractive, very variable but basically shaped like ivy, in deep green, marbled in light grey, pewter or even silver, with deep red undersides. In a temperate climate they endure the vagaries of winter weather and remain decorative until dormancy begins in late spring of the following year. They should be top-dressed with leaf mould or any organic mulch to encourage strong new growth. This cyclamen seeds in the most unpromising

Cyclamen repandum

Cyclamen hederifolium

Cyclamen coum

subspecies. In general it has plain green glossy rounded leaves but some have distinctive marblings. The short-stemmed flowers are white, pale pink or deep carmine, with a dark purple blotch at the base of each petal, and open in midwinter. Unlike *C. repandum* and *C. hederifolium*, *C. coum* prefers damp ground – it will thrive next to primroses. Though perhaps less exciting than the other two, it is still a worthwhile plant and it looks splendid massed, as in Lady Anne Rasch's garden at Heale House in Wiltshire. *C. cilicium* is a little trickier and needs more care, with gritty well-drained soil and protective mulches during dormancy. This autumn-flowering Turkish species is a delight, with small, elegantly shaped deep rose-pink flowers accompanied by spoon-shaped leaves.

Between them these cyclamen will provide decorative flowers or leaves to carpet the ground under larger plants at almost every season, only excepting a couple of months at midsummer, when most lose their deciduous leaves and become entirely dormant.

Cyclamen cilicium

places, thriving under deciduous shrubs and trees such as magnolias, but seemingly ready to germinate and flower even in the shade of a yew tree. It makes an ideal subject for growing at the shady base of an evergreen hedge, where almost nothing else except Welsh poppies would survive. At Tintinhull some of the tubers have grown to be almost 30cm/12in across and can occupy an inconvenient amount of space during the dormancy period in summer. I shall miss their maturity when I try to make a new garden. It can take fifty years or so to get cyclamen established and seeding as they do at Tintinhull.

There are two other cyclamen that I find especially useful in the garden. *C. coum*, which has a wide distribution in the wild in the Balkans and the Middle East, may well be an aggregate of many slightly variable

Onions in the Garden: the Alliums

MOST OF US grow alliums in the herb or vegetable garden as onions, chives or leeks. But that should be just the beginning. The allium family includes a vast number of species – something like a thousand in all – and the range used regularly in gardens could easily be much increased. Each year I get more enthusiastic about alliums, more aware of their garden possibilities and the pleasure one could have from growing more of the rarer kinds.

Members of the Liliaciae family, all alliums are perennial bulbs. Nearly all have a characteristic smell of garlic or onions and most bear umbels of tiny flowers packed closely together. Beyond that these plants are extremely variable. Coming from very diverse habitats, they have developed different traits. A large bulb, adapted for dormancy in a hot climate, generally signifies that an allium comes from a dry, arid habitat, while alliums from more temperate, cooler climates have smaller, slender bulbs, often clustered on a short rhizome – or indeed may appear to have a fibrous system. The leaves are equally divergent, sometimes short and erect, sometimes long and floppy or thin and thread-like. The leaves of the alliums from hot countries usually begin to fade before the plant comes into flower; those from damp upland meadows retain fresh leaves throughout the summer. Judicious selection can unearth candidates for most garden situations, from baking hot well-drained rockeries, where the dumpy *Allium karataviense* will thrive, displaying its splendid purplish glaucous leaves and pinkish-purple florets, to areas that are moist during the summer growing months, which are suitable for the late flowerers such

Allium aflatunense 'Purple Sensation'

as the distinguished greeny-white *A. tuberosum*. No allium, however, will long endure a location that is water-logged during the winter.

At Tintinhull we have never been very adventurous about alliums, partly because of the constraints of the original plant lists; however, we have added various alliums to most of the main borders, and some of these now seed themselves in happy abandon in other parts of the garden. Taking my ideas from what I saw at Sissinghurst, I started by introducing hardy drumstick varieties, with large globular heads of mauve florets, among and around shrub roses. One of the first we planted was *A. christophii* (*A. albopilosum*), with 20cm/8in diameter heads made up of blueish-violet starry florets held on rather stumpy short stalks (up to

40cm/16in). But I really prefer the taller alliums, finding them more graceful, and we soon added the late-flowering blue *A. caeruleum* (up to 80cm/32in), *A. rosenbachianum*, with 1m/3ft stems and violet star-shaped flowers held in a looser spherical umbel, and *A. aflatunense*, with heads of deep violet and stems running to about 1.5m/5ft.

There are many other desirable alliums for which we have never found space at Tintinhull, and I hope that I will have the opportunity to experiment with some of these in my new garden. I certainly plan to try magenta-flowered *A. polyastrum*, with star-shaped florets, *A. macranthum*, with plum-purple bell-shaped flowers, maroon-purple *A. wallichii* and *A. cernuum*, with pinkish flowers and almost evergreen leaves.

Allium christophii

Allium caeruleum

Allium cernuum

BEHIND THE SCENES

I N PRACTICAL TERMS the nitty and gritty side of garden work has no seasonal beginning or end, but there are two definite moments in the year when the rhythms change: in February, and in late June.

Chronologically, mid-February is the most practical moment to start the 'behind the scenes' year at Tintinhull. It is then that the days begin to lengthen perceptibly, and plants in the greenhouse or in cold frames put out new shoots. Adrenaline rises in the excitement of planning and discussing the spring and summer appearance of the garden for the year. And from February on, the 'behind the scenes' work of sowing, pricking out, rooting cuttings and potting on – traditional greenhouse tasks undertaken in preparation for the summer beauty of beds and containers – is almost as important as more obvious routine gardening.

As seeds germinate and plants need pricking out, greenhouses and frames get very full. In our first years at Tintinhull we had two small 3m × 2.5m/10ft × 8ft greenhouses; later we added a third. Two were used for work in progress, while the third, heated to only just above freezing, was for the larger pot plants which benefit from winter protection: cordylines, corokias, correas, *Dodonaea viscosa* 'Purpurea' (before it grew too large and had to stay in the summerhouse where it did not survive), leptospermums and olearias from New Zealand and Australia, myrtles from southern Europe, tender buddlejas and *Jasminum polyanthum* from Asia, *Melianthus major* and bomareas from South Africa, and the dahlia-like *Cosmos atrosanguineus*, both of the latter dormant in winter and needing no water. There were woody salvias and the choosy perennial velvety-flowered *Salvia buchananii* from Mexico, as well as favourites such as *S. clevelandii* from California, and lemon-scented verbena, *Aloysia triphylla* (*Lippia citriodora*), a traditional greenhouse plant in Britain, coming from Chile two centuries ago.

Cold frames are another essential, both for hardening off young plants before they go to their garden sites, and for winter-storing many of the hardiest rooted cuttings, as well as pots of *Francoa sonchifolia*, which sit on the steps in the Eagle Court, and pots of regale lilies for the summerhouse.

The greenhouse and cold frame area at Tintinhull is backed up by a good shed for tools and storage, and a wide potting bench. There are sheltered nursery beds for growing on, but over the years much of the available planting space has been filled with permanent small trees and shrubs, mostly Asiatic and grown from seed: magnolias; a tall *Ehretia dicksonii*; *Cladrastis sinensis*, which takes twenty years to flower; both *Rhus potaninii* and the varnish tree, *R. verniciflua*; *Phellodendron amurense*; *Tetradium daniellii* Hupehense Group (*Euodia hupehensis*); and a spreading *Aesculus parviflora* which flowers in July and August – all of which as they mature provide a 'borrowed' landscape of fine shape and foliage at the back of the garden wall behind the Cedar Court. Smaller woody plants fit into the experimental beds round the Kitchen Garden, and soft-stemmed perennials can be grown there in rows, encroaching on vegetable space.

If we buy in perennial plants – we usually add some new varieties when redoing a bed – we do not expect to be able to use them in a border the first year, but repot them in our own compost or put them out in the Kitchen Garden or our nursery area to grow on for the summer.

WINTER INTO SPRING

As daylight hours lengthen, winter pruning and tidying – even if unfinished – give way to sowing and propagating.

Although we mix our own compost for our big pots (see page 203) we do not find it worthwhile to make up our own mix for seed or for growing on or cuttings; it is too time-consuming. Instead we buy in appropriate proprietary composts. All of those we use contain loam, peat and sand, and a slow-release fertilizer. We have tried using alternatives without peat, such as coir (processed coconut fibre), but we find that they dry out quickly, and young plants need feeding almost immediately. We use plastic trays for seeds, and I prefer square pots for plants that are potted on individually, as round containers take up more space. All must be scrupulously washed after use, and they should be stored in the dark or they will become brittle.

Left: *Some time in winter I examine all my bags of seed, shake their contents on to a saucer and remove any debris. Then I pour the seeds into small polythene or paper envelopes which are stored in silica gel in the refrigerator.*

Right: *The greenhouses in spring are packed with tender plants, potted on from rooted cuttings, and seedlings pricked out from the initial sowing a few weeks earlier.*

All our seeds, whether of annuals, trees, shrubs or perennials, are sown during February and March, and these will include seeds collected in the garden, as well as interesting seeds obtained on my travels (fortunately, seed does not need a phytosanitary certificate), or treasured seeds sent by friends in the States and elsewhere – the new introductions widening the range and interest of plants in the garden. In the autumn we make lists of all the seeds we have gathered, and again work out how many plants we will need for the garden schemes.

Recently, as the garden filled up, most of the trees and shrubs grown from seed at Tintinhull have been given away. But in our earlier years here there was still space for small trees such as the St Lucie cherry (*Prunus mahaleb*), *Aesculus californica* (grown from seed sent by a friend in the International Dendrology Society), and the evergreen *Maytenus boqria* from Chile. Many others grown from seed were planted in my husband John's arboretum in the orchard.

Annuals are a vital element in the garden. They need three months' growing time, to make strong root systems, before being planted out. They will be potted on three or four times during this interval, and will be planted out after the last frost, towards the end of May – or even later, as tulips and forget-me-nots finish and make space in the beds or containers.

We grow mostly species rather than nursery hybrid annuals, but also try new varieties offered by seedsmen. Our own seed includes that of tobacco plants such as *Nicotiana langsdorffii, N. sylvestris*, and the grey-leaved South American *N. glauca*, which may reach 2.5m/8ft in a summer. Tobacco plants often self-hybridize to produce interesting variations. We also germinate seed of a few plants which nearly always seed *in situ*, just as an insurance: *Collomia debilis* with apricot flowers; the bright pink *Silene armeria;* the miniature *Polygonum capitatum*, which is allowed to trail over the stones which flank the Pool Garden borders; red and orange Chilean glory-flowers, *Eccremocarpus scaber;* and the square-stemmed mauve *Verbena bonariensis*.

Many of the soft-stemmed tender sages are also grown from seed (the more woody ones are propagated from cuttings). The intense blue *Salvia patens* and the pale 'Cambridge Blue' and mauve 'Chilcombe' germinate easily but dislike being pricked out, so we usually grow them in peat pots to prevent root disturbance. The related *Lepechinia salviae*, with dusky red flowers, and *Lobelia tupa*, with maroon flowers, are treated in the same way.

Seeds of the blue-flowered *Lathyrus sativus* and cream *Hibiscus trionum* are sown for the Pool Garden pots, *Dahlia merckii* for the Kitchen Garden, where it may self-seed in another year, and *Rehmannia elata*, with its strange hooded flowers, for the beds by the summerhouse. The biennial giant thistle, *Onopordum acanthium*, important for its sculptural appearance in the foliage garden at the back of the Fountain Garden, is sown for flowering the following summer, as is the milk thistle, *Silybum marianum*, to go in an odd corner, and Miss Willmott's ghost, *Eryngium giganteum*, for the Pool Garden beds, while white foxgloves can always be fitted in on the north side of the house.

We germinate seeds of hardier perennials and woody plants in case clumps or specimens need renewing after the winter. The sprawling catmint, *Nepeta nervosa*, at the base of the pink 'Mevrouw Nathalie Nypels' roses in the Kitchen Garden needs replacing almost annually; it gets squeezed out by neighbouring plants. More plants of the perennial peas, salmon-coloured *Lathyrus rotundifolius*, and Lord Anson's treasured blue pea, *L. nervosus*, are always welcome.

The seed of *Perilla frutescens* var. *crispa* with dusky purple leaves, which is so perfect for the hot border in the Pool Garden, like that of the blue hyacinth bean, *Lablab purpureus* (*Dolichos lablab*) – of which we need six plants to grow on tripods in the Kitchen Garden – rarely ripens in Britain's cool summers, so I ask for seed each year from friends in the States. Also from the States comes seed for different American eupatoriums and vernonias (from a gardener in Pennsylvania), amsonias – which we have found difficult to establish – and *Baptisia australis*, with blue pea flowers and beautiful black pods; as well as some more Mexican and Californian salvias, most of which are kept in individual pots. We buy in seeds of Swan river daisy (*Brachyscome*), sweet peas for the house, and vegetables for the Kitchen Garden.

Cuttings of tender shrubby plants that will be treated as annuals are taken from overwintered stock plants as they recommence growth. These, when rooted, will replace plants that were rooted the previous August or September and which, in spite of being overwintered in the cold frames, look unhealthy or have not survived. We check how many of each plant we need for all the garden sites, but always grow a few extra. Plants will include anisodonteas, argyranthemums, artemisias, diascias, felicias, osteospermums and penstemons. Also included will be some of the most important featured plants at Tintinhull, such as *Artemisia* 'Powis Castle' and *Argyranthemum foeniculaceum*, both of which have rapidly expanding root systems and need frequent potting on. And in addition to this, some cuttings of rarer shrubs that have been in the main mist propagator through the winter (with heat and water turned off) will now need potting up.

I enjoy gardening with tender but fast-growing plants. They can either be grouped with hardy perennials and shrubs in the beds, or kept in containers. As the garden at Tintinhull has grown together, there has been less room for tender plants and annuals between the

Above, left and right: *In early spring the dead leaves of the hellebores are tidied away, so that they look at their best when in flower. We also spread a mulch around their crowns and between the clumps to set off the flowers and young leaves.*

permanent planting, and more need for pots. I hope to continue experimenting with them at Bettiscombe.

Potted cuttings that have rooted in the late summer start to grow again in February, and quickly get root-bound unless they are re-potted. They may need further potting by the end of March, which allows them six weeks or so to get well established in their new containers in cold frames before being planted out. We use quite a few anisodonteas, argyranthemums, mimulus, osteospermums, penstemons, and my favourite blue salvias, *Salvia cacaliifolia*, *S. guaranitica*, *S. leptophylla* and *S. leucantha*. All these are grown from cuttings, like the more woody sages – the scarlet *S. fulgens* and *S. coccinea*, destined for the hot border in the Pool Garden, the black-flowered *S. discolor* for the summerhouse pots, and forms of *S. microphylla* for the hot borders or for containers.

Ideally, labels for all these plants will have been prepared on wet or freezing winter days, but so many tasks are kept for bad weather that this is seldom achieved. Labelling, however, is essential.

Some outside tasks are also vital February chores, the background to success later in the year. Digging the vegetable garden should be completed as early as possible, and pruning of late-summer buddlejas and small-flowered clematis must be fitted in by the end of the month. If this is done earlier in the winter, unseasonable warm spells may encourage shoots which will be damaged by frosts; if left too late, flowering will be delayed.

Late frosts can damage buds of quite mature plants – early-flowering magnolias, and hydrangeas, such as *Hydrangea aspera* Villosa Group, which do not flower until late summer. The new shoots of young shrubs are also particularly vulnerable, and those still with a small root system may not recover from a hard frost in

April or May. When frosts threaten, it is worth throwing a loose covering of net or fleece over the most vulnerable shrubs – and also over the growing tips of lilies.

In March, all the roses, except for the Scotch burnets, need attention. Bush roses, already trimmed back in November to prevent wind rock, are properly pruned (see pages 152–3). Large shrub roses have their old or dead wood cut out from the base during the winter, but in March any frost-tipped shoots should be removed. Their arching graceful shapes, so valuable in the garden, are easily spoilt if they are wrongly pruned, and branches should only be cut back by a third or so. The most back-breaking rose-pruning at Tintinhull is in the bed of massed apothecary's rose, *Rosa gallica* var. *officinalis*, in the Kitchen Garden. Each shoot needs cutting back to two buds above ground level. It might be worth experimenting, and using hedge clippers or even a strimmer to cut back more ruthlessly.

As soon as rose leaves unfurl, a two-weekly spraying programme against blackspot, mildew and aphids is essential. Use any good rose mixture. Peony tips and lily shoots, both subject to botrytis, can also benefit from being sprayed with a fungicide as they appear.

Spring weeding is followed by mulching with any organic homemade compost or a mushroom compost that we obtain locally. (We hardly ever use farmyard manure, which produces a whole crop of weed seeds.) This will effectively retain moisture in the soil throughout the drier summer months, as well as suppressing weed germination. I try not to mulch where annuals are to go until after they have been planted, then I spread the mulch all around them. It acts as a valuable cosmetic and sets off the young growth of all plants in an attractive workmanlike way.

In March, the hellebores in the north-facing bed in the Eagle Court and under the magnolias in the Cedar Court need their dead leaves cutting away. Then they are mulched. Seedlings which have germinated around their stems are noted, to be dug up later; these, probably mixed offspring of different parents, can be potted up for use in other areas of the garden, or grown on to see if they have any special flower colour or shape.

Sowing Seeds

AT TINTINHULL most seeds are sown in February, in half-trays of a suitable seed compost. It is important that the compost should be thoroughly moist. I usually hold the tray in water, almost level with the rim, until all air-bubbles disappear. Then I take it out and press down on it with another tray to level the soil (*below left*). Seed should be scattered quite thinly on the surface of the compost (*below centre*). With very fine seed it may be worth mixing it with sand to ensure a more even distribution. In most cases a thin layer of sieved compost is then shaken over the seeds. However, some seeds, such as those of tobacco plants, prefer to germinate in the light on the surface, and they are left completely uncovered. Others need to be kept in the dark; they can be covered with a layer of glass and newspaper until they have germinated. We place the labelled seed trays on top of the heated soil in the mist propagator, but without the mist in operation.

After germination, as soon as the seedlings are large enough to be handled, they are pricked out into a richer growing compost in larger trays. Generally the seedlings are ready when the second lot of leaves appears. If you can, pot them on with a little soil attached to the wispy roots. Scoop a little clump out of the tray and gently separate them, holding them by the leaves to avoid clasping the fragile stems, then gently firm them into the compost (*right, top to bottom*). We keep our seedlings in the frost-free greenhouse for another few weeks and then harden them off, first in closed frames and later in frames without lids, so that they are well acclimatized before being put out in their flowering sites. During their time in the greenhouse they need little but frequent watering – a gentle spray two or three times a day rather than a good soak – and should be protected from the hot midday sun. The trays will keep damp by capillary action if placed on moist sand or gravel.

SPRING INTO SUMMER

All through March, April and the first half of May, greenhouses and frames need monitoring. Hot sun can decimate small seedlings, and unexpected frosts, if windows or frame lids are left open, can ruin a whole crop of seeds or cuttings. As the weather warms up the frames can be left open more and more, unless a frost is threatened. It is worth listening to the weather forecast during this anxious period, as one hard frost can do a lot of damage. Plants should never go straight from a greenhouse into the ground but must have a hardening-off period in frames.

In the last half of March and throughout April, perennials that have not been dealt with in the autumn are dug up, split and moved to new sites which have been planned since the end of the previous summer. This gives a chance to fork in compost and prepare the ground more effectively; we only dig when a whole border is renovated. Achilleas, cephalarias, *Clematis recta*, crambes, the white epilobium, eupatoriums, galegas, *Lysimachia ciliata* 'Purpurea', phygelius and veronicastrums are all natural spreaders, and need controlling rather than frequent dividing. Phlox should be lifted at least every three or four years, the central root crown thrown away, and young plants from the outer edge reused. *Aster × frikartii* 'Mönch' should be renewed by cuttings every few seasons.

In April there is still plenty of garden tidying to do: leaves to be swept up, paving to sweep, gravel to rake in the Kitchen Garden, lawns that need feeding and levelling. There are also urgent tasks to prevent trouble a year later. We have very few perennial weeds but, of course, dandelion and thistle seed is always blowing in from the outlying orchards. Another persistent weed is the attractive perennial arum with smooth green leaves, known as lords and ladies and cousin to *Arum italicum* 'Marmoratum'.

In the main beds and borders weeds are easily spotted, but in the more informal parts of the garden they tend to be overlooked. Annual weeds include the little creeping veronica, *Veronica hederifolia*, pretty with its blue flowers, but extremely persistent, colonizing where it can, and quickly overrunning early-flowering anemones and scillas. It needs weeding out by hand where it germinates all over the garden. This sort of weeding is relatively skilled, as garden plants and seedlings are also appearing, sometimes in unexpected places. We have lost a lot of plants from hasty work done by willing but inexperienced hands.

In April and May, established herbaceous perennials need mulching as they appear, and staking is done in May. We keep this to a minimum, giving support only to the most unruly plants, up to a third of their expected height. We always try to get coppiced hazel, but often have to make do with bamboos and string and some of the circular metal supports. The fast-growing twining clematis all need attention throughout April, May and June: their shoots carefully guided to fan out or clamber into neighbouring shrubs in order to prevent unsightly birds' nest effects.

We prune evergreen trees and shrubs, except for yew and box hedges, in April or May. If they are done any later, there is a danger that new growth made late in the year will be vulnerable to hard

The wild arums are among the most irritating weeds at Tintinhull. We try to dig them out but often break off the stems without getting out the whole root system. In some parts of the garden I occasionally use a contact weedkiller to weaken their growth.

Left: *We have to keep on top of pulling out the annual weeds which germinate as the ground heats up in spring. Most of our weeding is done by hand. I use a hand-cultivator to freshen up the soil but we never use a hoe in the flower beds, as precious seedlings might be lost.*

Below: *In late spring we have the pleasure and excitement of taking plants from the greenhouses and cold frames and putting them out in their permanent positions in the borders. The photographs show new plants of* Coronilla valentina *ssp* glauca *and* Abutilon × suntense *to go in the Eagle Court.*

winter frosts. Winter-flowering laurustinus (forms of *Viburnum tinus*), osmanthus – which needs little formal pruning – itea, rhamnus, and low-growing lavenders and cotton lavenders all need cutting to make good shapes. Spring-flowering viburnums, choisyas, *Osmanthus delavayi* and more tender olearias and other New Zealanders are tidied back after flowering is over. Only the summer-flowering shrubs are left untouched.

During the last ten days of May and the first weeks of June, dead tulip leaves are removed, and some of the bulbs dug up to make space. By now, most of the new plants – annuals and tender shrubs used as annuals – are well hardened off and ready to put out in their permanent sites. Some, such as diascias and lobelias, have already been planted out, earlier in the month. Before planting, all the trays and pots of plants are held in a tank of water until air-bubbles cease to appear. This is always a good idea, but is particularly important for these quick-maturing short-season plants which have to start growing into their sites at once. Where possible, and if there is enough space between neighbouring plants, we prepare the ground by forking it over and incorporating organic compost. I also like to add a handful of dried organic fertilizer to each planting hole. All these plants are heavy feeders, producing a great number of flowers in only a few months.

Some of the plants go in planters of one kind or another, and here soil conditions are more easily controlled. We mix compost for the larger pots, using a mixture of soil taken from the Kitchen Garden, sand and peat. We also add slow-release fertilizer and granules of a water-storing non-toxic gel which swells to make water available to plants' roots throughout periods of drought. The gel is effective for up to five seasons, and much reduces the need to water.

In June, the garden reaches its first flowering peak, with roses and early-flowering perennials. But this is also the beginning of the garden cycle in real terms. During the next months we will be taking seed, making cuttings, and generally undertaking much of the preparation for the garden display of the following year.

Taking Seed

I BEGIN TAKING SEED of perennials, biennials and annuals as soon as any of it is ripe, usually in July. Annuals and biennials are the most important of the seed crops, but we generally take seed of quite a few of the less reliably hardy perennials in case we should have a bad winter.

Seed should be gathered on a dry sunny day, never when it is wet, as it rots very easily. The seed of many flowers, such as the little cream-flowered *Hibiscus trionum*, *Francoa sonchifolia*, greenish-yellow *Nicotiana langsdorffii* and *Salvia patens*, is ripe when it is black and dry, just before the container splits open to distribute it. That of others, such as lathyrus and beans, is contained in pods, and is ready for gathering when the seeds have swollen and the pod itself is completely dry. Yet others have fruit-like outer cases, with the seed protected and hidden inside: seed of these plants, such as *Tropaeolum speciosum*, bomareas and solanums, is gathered when the outer layer begins to dry out. The perennial honesty, *Lunaria rediviva*, has transparent capsules, and seed is ripe

when black (*above left*). I take seed of this only occasionally, as seedlings germinate freely around the established plants.

Seed should be collected in paper bags (it can be stored in plastic after it is fully dry, but not before). I keep fairly large bags from household shopping for this purpose, labelling them carefully with the plant name and the date (*above right*). The bags are then stored somewhere dry, until a winter day when I find the opportunity to clean and sort the seed.

The annual *Hibiscus trionum*, which grows in the Pool Garden, in large pots around the pool, has capsules containing about eight seeds, which I cut off and drop into a bag (*below left*). *Nicotiana langsdorffii*, another annual, has fine seed which can be squeezed out straight into a bag, as can the

similar seed of the perennial *Francoa sonchifolia*. I always collect seed of francoa, in case we lose the parent plants in the cold frame where they overwinter. Most salvia seed is easy to gather: the capsules, each containing one ripe seed, should be pinched to prevent the seed jumping out, then eased off the plant and dropped into a bag (*below centre*). The upward-facing decorative heads of love-in-a-mist, *Nigella damascena*, are gathered in August. If the heads are turned upside down, the seed can be rubbed out into a bag (*below right*). I sometimes save time by cutting off whole flower heads of large thistles, and some of the taller tobacco plants, dropping them straight into the bags for later cleaning and sorting. They can also be hung upside down in their bags, so that the seed falls out as it dries.

Taking Cuttings

CUTTINGS AT TINTINHULL fall into several categories. Every year we take cuttings of plants that may not be reliably hardy, such as abutilon, piptanthus, leptospermums, cistus and the more tender roses. We take a large number of cuttings each year of the tender woody plants that we treat as annuals and of softer-stemmed plants that are used for bedding or containers. These two latter categories include diascias, felicias, woody and soft-stemmed salvias, argyranthemums and anisodonteas. We take woody cuttings from shrubs such as berberis, box, deutzias and spiraeas simply for future replacement of old plants. For most shrubs cuttings are taken when new growth has begun to firm up, probably in midsummer. We take clematis cuttings later in the summer. We also take spring cuttings of perennials, to avoid the bother of division, and of overwintered tender stock plants, to take the pressure off greenhouse space in the winter. Very often heeled cuttings of new growth give appropriate material, but longer branches can be cut up between the nodes to give a number of suitable shoots.

We always take heeled cuttings of tender *Salvia cacaliifolia*, one of the best performers in pots (*left and below left*). Shoots root most easily if taken from a non-flowering branch but this is sometimes difficult to find. Keep the cuttings in an airtight plastic bag and pot them up as soon as possible, following the method described on pages 82–3. In the mist propagator *S. cacaliifolia* cuttings root in a few weeks, but care is needed – this salvia is liable to die off during the winter if over-watered. After the roots are formed the plants are potted individually and overwintered in the greenhouse. They are usually ready to be potted on to larger containers in early spring. The young plants are hardened off in frames before being planted out in full sun.

S. leucantha (*below centre*) flowers later than *S. cacaliifolia* – in warmer climates than ours it will flower all winter. Cuttings can be rooted any time after midsummer.

Some plants, including *Argyranthemum foeniculaceum*, have a very quick-growing root system. With these, as well as taking summer cuttings (*below right*), we generally keep a few stock plants in the greenhouse over the winter and take cuttings of young shoots which grow as the daylight hours lengthen in February.

SUMMER INTO WINTER

From June on, repeat-flowering roses must have their dead heads regularly removed, and others, unless they have attractive fruits, also need unsightly dead blooms taken off. Perennials need deadheading, and in some cases cutting down to the ground in order to encourage new foliage growth. In spite of mulching, we need to keep a look out for weeds, and any purple-flowered foxgloves that appear should be removed before the bees can cross-fertilize with the white ones. (The purple-flowered ones can be identified before they flower by their purple-tinged stems.)

Behind the scenes, seeds of hardy biennials, such as forget-me-nots or winter- and spring-flowering pansies, need sowing in rows in the Kitchen Garden (see page 110). They will be transplanted to their garden sites by the end of September, while the earth is still warm enough for their roots to establish. June is almost the last moment for germinating most biennials outside, from the previous year's seeds, if they are to flower the following year, though some – *Eryngium giganteum*, *Salvia sclarea* var. *turkestanica* and foxgloves among them – may flower the following year if seed is sown *in situ* as soon as it is ripe at the end of July. All can, of course, be raised more easily from seed in the greenhouse in spring, to flower the following year. These seeders are not individually the most important flowers in the garden, but collectively their seeming spontaneity when scattered in drifts through many of the flower beds is part of the Tintinhull look – the 'jungle of beauty' effect.

Around the end of June, the rhythm changes to a more contemplative spiral. As the chores of deadheading, cutting off dead leaves, and watering proceed, thoughts fly to the following year. It is possible to contemplate and consider the garden in a way that cannot be done during the rushed spring and early summer. It is a period for reflection and optimism, with the promise always of doing better next year – every gardener's dream.

With all mixed planting, many of the permanently planted soft-stemmed plants need an annual reshuffle in order to keep both the colour sequence and the proportions of neighbouring plant groups in scale. Taking photographs while performance is at its peak – in June, July, August and September – helps ensure that replanting achieves the desired effects the following year.

The garden must be kept well groomed before the 'dog days' of August, when garden plants can quickly look shabby. Late-flowering plants need to be accompanied by tidy neighbours. It is vital to deadhead not only roses but also irises and early-flowering perennials: columbines (mainly blue forms of *Aquilegia vulgaris*, a flowerer allowed all over the garden), the acid-yellow bracts of *Smyrnium perfoliatum* (leaving some to set seed), and the invasive Welsh poppy, *Meconopsis cambrica*, which will otherwise colonize the garden and be almost impossible to weed out. Summer-flowering shrubs such as lilac, philadelphus, deutzias, sambucus and

Above, left and right: Some alchemilla plants have been allowed to seed in the cracks of stonework. After flowering, alchemilla stems and foliage should be cut right back. The plants will then produce attractive mounds of fresh foliage.

viburnums all have their flowering branches cut out after flowering, to allow new growth on which flowers will be produced next year, and when the dead heads and long stems of the big euphorbias (varieties of *Euphorbia characias* and *E.c.* ssp. *wulfenii*) become unsightly in July, they should be cut back to the hidden base. The large heart-shaped leaves of tall crambes can also look faded, and should be trimmed back, leaving the flower sprays which remain decorative in seed. Long, rooting stems of *Buglossoides purpurocaerulea* can be cut back to the ground in July and August; if it is a dry summer this will be sufficient, but in wet years they will have to be trimmed again if cut too early. During August, crane's-bill geraniums, galegas and alchemillas can be cut back to the ground. Some of the geraniums will flower again, though not the alchemillas or galegas. All will produce new leaves that will last until autumn.

Cuttings of permanent shrubs, which need to be taken from young half-ripened shoots that are not too soft, can be rooted in the mist propagator in late July and in August. Rose shoots taken in July are easily rooted in mist (see page 111), although they can also be grown from hardwood cuttings set in a trench in winter. Cuttings of tender plants to be used as annuals can be taken in July and August from non-flowering shoots. By early September this task should be completed.

August and September bring new bursts of bloom from perennials, and we make a note to increase the range and number of hydrangeas that we know Mrs Reiss loved. Over the years many have disappeared, and this would be a good time to beg cuttings from friends. On the other hand, we have added a lot of other late

flowerers to those, such as evening primroses, hollyhocks, ceanothus and hydrangeas, already in the garden: eupatoriums, chelones (copying the Powis Castle borders), cimicifugas, vernonias, veronicastrums – all of which help to disguise the fading stems of the earlier-flowering herbaceous planting. Some cutting back is necessary to set off these late performers. Other efforts go into collecting the seeds we will need for the garden next year.

A beautiful evergreen privet, *Ligustrum quihoui*, with white panicles 20in/50cm long, flowers now in a quiet border where earlier the beauty bush, *Kolkwitzia amabilis*, reigned supreme. The kolkwitzia has had its long flowering fronds cut back to make a shapely bush and to ensure new growth for next year's flowers.

Gardening work becomes more intense again in September. The autumn months are for clearing up and reassessment; for carrying out major tasks of reorganization, for scarifying the lawn, and for pruning shrubs that flower on next year's new shoots, as soon as they are dormant.

Autumn work is vital: moving shrubs as necessary and as they become dormant, and cutting down perennials – but leaving those, such as sedums and grasses, with flowers and leaves which continue to look handsome through the autumn months. Spent annuals must be pulled out, and the last seed gathered and stored. Some of the groups of the hardiest perennials are split and reshuffled now when there is more time than in the spring – though a danger is a wet autumn followed by early hard frosts which freeze water around their newly moved crowns.

Major reconstruction of borders can begin in September. This allows time for digging the beds over. If sterilization is needed, to rid soil of harmful pests and diseases, as well as any build-up of weed seeds, this is the time to do it, while the soil is still warm. Over the years we have had to sterilize the soil in various of the Tintinhull borders, against rose replant diseases. Soil sterilization is not a job for the amateur. The fumigants used are toxic and can only be employed by commercial growers and approved contractors,

who take every precaution in their handling. Borders have to be cleared of perennials, though shrubs can usually be left. Then the professionals apply the fumigant (in volatile liquid or powder form) and seal the surface of the soil with plastic sheeting to retain the vapours. After autumn sterilization woody plants can be replanted in winter and perennials in the following spring.

Throughout October, November and December leaves are swept up and carefully removed from flower beds in which they might 'overlay' emerging shoots of winter or spring flowerers, causing the crowns to rot. For this reason, the large leaves of *Magnolia liliiflora* 'Nigra' are raked up as they fall, on an almost daily basis. Depending on the weather, the lawns need occasional mowing and edging up until Christmas.

Other winter chores include checking and cleaning tools, tidying sheds, checking the watering systems, writing labels for seed trays, and checking lists of plants required for the following season. By February the year's new season begins.

The white epilobium, Epilobium angustifolium album, *is only cut down as the lower leaves begin to look unsightly, at the very end of the season, long after flowering and producing seedheads.*

INDEX

Page numbers in *italic* type refer to illustrations and their captions and to planting plans. For an explanation of hardiness zones, e.g. **Z8**, see page 215.

HARDINESS ZONES

The hardiness zone ratings given for each plant – indicated in the index by the letter **Z** and the relevant number – suggest the appropriate minimum temperature a plant will tolerate in winter. The zone ratings are based on those devised by the United States Department of Agriculture. The chart below shows the average annual minimum temperature of each zone.

Zoning data can only be a rough guide. Hardiness depends on a great many factors, including the depth of a plant's roots, its water content at the onset of frost, the duration of cold weather, the force of the wind, and the length of, and temperatures encountered during, the preceding summer. Zone ratings given here are allocated to plants according to their tolerance of winter cold in the British Isles and Western Europe. In climates with hotter and/or drier summers, as in Australia and New Zealand, some plants will survive colder temperatures and their hardiness in these countries may occasionally be one, or even rarely two, zones lower than that quoted.

Most of the British Isles lies within Zone 8, with the exception of the western and southern coasts and central London, which are Zone 9, and the Highlands of Scotland, which are Zone 7.

CELSIUS	ZONES	°FAHRENHEIT
below -45	1	below -50
-45 to -40	2	-50 to -40
-40 to -34	3	-40 to -30
-34 to -29	4	-30 to -20
-29 to -23	5	-20 to -10
-23 to -18	6	-10 to 0
-18 to -12	7	0 to 10
-12 to -7	8	10 to 20
-7 to -1	9	20 to 30
-1 to 4	10	30 to 40
above 4	11	above 40

ACKNOWLEDGMENTS

AUTHOR'S ACKNOWLEDGMENTS

The idea for this book, originally conceived to be descriptive of Tintinhull and to be written with my late husband, John Malins, came from Frances Lincoln and Erica Hunningher. The present form, more of a personal odyssey, evolved in discussion. We knew from the start that the book would be nothing without Andrew Lawson's pictures: he had been taking the garden over the years and agreed to photograph both there and elsewhere especially for the book. I am most grateful to the garden owners who generously allowed their gardens to be photographed.

Looking after the garden at Tintinhull was a partnership with my husband, John, whose knowledge and gardening wisdom held the garden together. We were wonderfully helped by the skill and dedicated work of Bert Austin and Glynn Jones, the two National Trust gardeners, who, in succession, covered most of our fourteen years. I wish the new gardener, now totally in charge of the garden, great success and happiness in caring for it.

The Frances Lincoln team have as always been inspired and methodical: Jo Christian, my editor, Caroline Hillier, the art director, and Anne Fraser, the picture editor. Tony Lord's encyclopedic knowledge of plant names and their up-to-the-minute changes make the book a reliable guide to current nomenclature. I am very grateful to everyone who has been involved.

PUBLISHERS' ACKNOWLEDGMENTS

Frances Lincoln Limited are grateful to the National Trust for their cooperation. The publishers also wish to offer special thanks to Antonia Johnson, Katherine Lambert and Caroline Taylor for their help in producing this book.

Plan script by Simon Johnson

Design by Studio Gossett

Horticultural consultant Tony Lord
Editor Jo Christian
Picture Editor Anne Fraser
Indexer Penny David
Production Adela Cory
Design assistance Sally Cracknell
Editorial assistance Auriol Miller

Editorial Director Erica Hunningher
Art Director Caroline Hillier
Production Director Nicky Bowden

PHOTOGRAPHIC ACKNOWLEDGMENTS

a = above, b = below, c = centre, l = left, r = right

All photographs copyright © Andrew Lawson, except for the following:
Deni Bown: 138bl, 145br, 174br, 175bc, 180al
Neil Campbell-Sharp: 24, 34ar
John Fielding: 145bc, 174bl, 180b (*Hoheria*), 192b, 193r
Jerry Harpur: 14, 23, 40-41, 149a, 168
Georges Lévêque © FLL: 39, 83a, 94